*More from Our Village of*

# Spencers Wood

# More from Our Village of

# Spencers Wood

Spencers Wood ✿ Local History Group

Spencers Wood Local History Group is a non-profit making group dedicated to researching and publishing local history in and around the village of Spencers Wood, Berkshire. All profits from sales of this book will be used to support further research and publishing.

This book would not have been possible without the contributions of residents of Spencers Wood, past and present. Our work is never finished. We would love to see any photos, memories, title deeds or other documents pertaining to the area, which you would be prepared to share with us.

Find us on the Web at swlhg.co.uk
Contact us at spwood.localhistory@googlemail.com

We are grateful to the team at Carnegie Book Production for their help in making our words and images look so smart, and we particularly thank Rachel Clarke for her patience and invaluable expertise.

Cover illustrations: *Front, top*: Village Hall chimney; Wellingtonia Drive, Stanbury; Highlands, 1970s (photo: Roy Bramley); Church of St Michael and all Angels; 'A moment in time during the war' (photo donated by Andy Skipp). *Bottom*: typical Spencers Wood brickwork; Clares Green SANG; photo of Edwardian lady and girl.
*Back*: aerial view of The Square, 1931 © Historic England; detail of F. W. Allfrey's Infants' School; window in the former Congregational Church.
(All colour photos by members of SWLHG.)

Published by Spencers Wood Local History Group

Copyright © Spencers Wood Local History Group (2016)

ISBN: 978-1-5272-0272-6

Cover design by Catherine Glover

Design and layout by Carnegie Book Production, Lancaster
www.carnegiepublishing.com
www.scotforthbooks.com

Printed and bound in Great Britain by TJ International Ltd, Padstow, Cornwall

# Contents

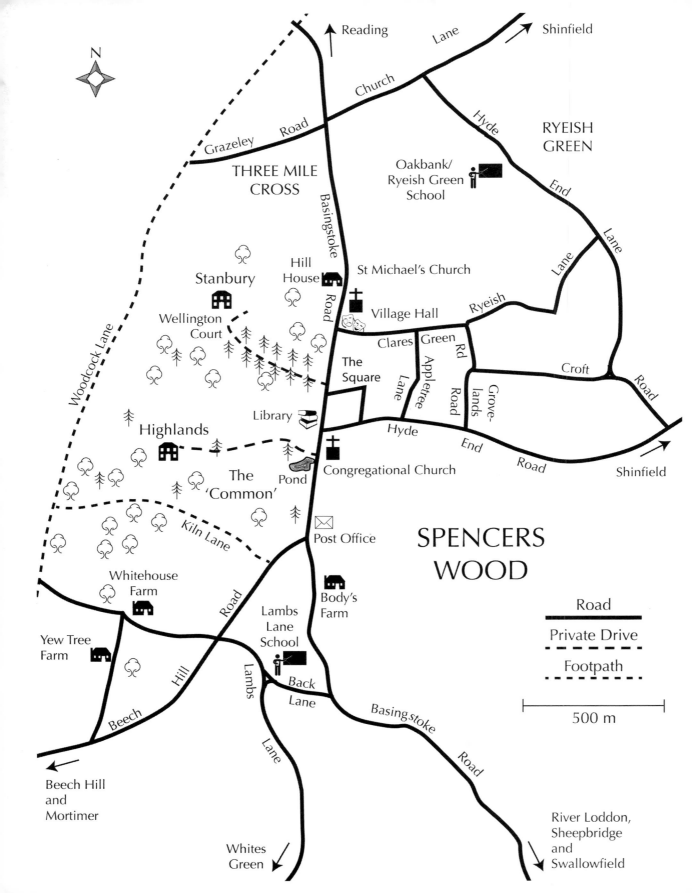

# Preface

Imagine the aspect from the crest of the hill above Three Mile Cross as Mary Russell Mitford (1787–1855) might have seen it: a long, straight road crossing a wide, flat heath; a few cottages left and right about half a mile away; and in the distance to the right a big modern house called Highlands, approached by a drive over the heath. By the side of the road on the left a scatter of cottages and part way, just after a pond on the left and before another on the right, a milestone: Reading 4, Basingstoke 12, Southampton 42. The milestone is still there, perhaps the sole remnant of these times. There was doubtless gorse to be seen on the heath, but also avenues of trees giving something of the feel of a park. This was Spencers Wood common. It extended as far as Kingsbridge in Swallowfield. Until 1844 it was in a detached portion of the county of Wiltshire. Shinfield parish covered Swallowfield, Grazeley and Beech Hill. In 1847, Swallowfield parish was separated out from Shinfield and in 1850 Grazeley followed, both becoming parishes in their own right. This meant that Spencers Wood common extended into three parishes and two counties: Wiltshire and Berkshire. After the enclosure acts of the 1850s and '60s, the common no longer legally existed, although today the land on the western side of Basingstoke Road, south of its junction with Hyde End Road retains an open aspect grazed by horses, with a public footpath across it, and we still refer to it as the 'Common'.

There was a non-conformist chapel in Spencers Wood from the beginning of the nineteenth century and a school from 1890: both feature in this book. In 1908 Henry Lannoy Hunter (1836–1909), the last of his name of Beech Hill House, gave the land on which the church of St Michael and All Angels was built, and in 1911 his wife had the Village Hall built in his memory, as St Michael's Hall. In 1913, Spencers Wood became an ecclesiastical parish, but for administrative purposes it remains in the civil parish of Shinfield; most of the village is also in the Shinfield ward of Wokingham Borough, except for the part south of the junction of Hyde End Road and Basingstoke Road, which is in Swallowfield Ward. The Recreation Ground was given to Shinfield Parish by Alexander Cobham of Shinfield Place, and this area – St Michael's Church, the Village Hall, and the Recreation Ground – represents the centre of 'Our Village of Spencers Wood'.

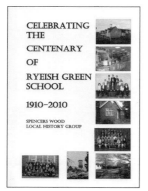

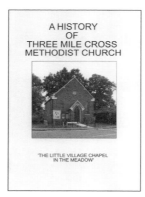

Since 1996, when Jeremy Saunders founded Spencers Wood Local History Group, we have produced four books and a Web site. The first book, which was entitled *Our Village of Spencers Wood* – to echo Mary Russell Mitford's *Our Village* (five volumes, published between 1824 and 1832) – was written by Margaret Bampton, Jackie Blow, Barbara Debney and Jill Sylvester. There followed two centenary books, *A History of Lambs Lane School, 1908–2008* and *Celebrating the Centenary of Ryeish Green School, 1910–2010* and lastly, *A History of Three Mile Cross Methodist Church* (which is just to the north of Spencers Wood), written by Patricia Green helped by Mary Wheway. On our Web site (www.swlhg.co.uk) you can find pictures, memories, links and all the articles we write for *Loddon Reach* magazine. Some of our members have passed on, and new ones have joined us. Shortly before publication we accepted the kind offer of another resident of Spencers Wood, Professor Richard Hoyle, to write the history of the common and its enclosure, and this he has done quite magnificently. We thank him heartily.

We also thank all of those who have directly or indirectly told us of their memories, and lent or given us their precious artefacts. This book reveals a community spirit that revolves around a vibrant Church and Village Hall: long may it continue. If you would like to contribute to further research in any way, please get in touch with us. The research and production of this book would not have been possible without the hard work and co-operation of the whole group. We hope you enjoy reading it as much as we have enjoyed producing it.

Whatever changes happen as a result of the current new housing developments, Mary Russell Mitford's beloved Common is still there underneath and the village has kept its rural feel.

Jackie Blow and Margaret Bampton

## CHAPTER ONE

# Before the Village

*Richard Hoyle*

Come to Spencers Wood, look around you, and there is no wood. Trees yes, often ornamental trees, but no wood. So was there ever a wood? And if so, where was it? And what happened to it? The first of these questions we can answer here: the others must wait.

In 1500 a Swallowfield man called John Blunt made his will. He made the usual sorts of bequests for the benefit of his soul. He left cows to his children, and made arrangements for the future ownership of a house in Reading. Of greater interest to us is the fact that he left 3*s*. 4*d*. for the repair of the road through the wood called Spencers Wood.[1] This is, for the moment, the earliest reference to Spencers Wood, and it confirms that there was at that time a wood there. By the time of the first adequate map of the area – that by John Rocque in 1761, reproduced on p. 5 – there was no wood as such. Instead there was a common, one of a series of commons and greens to the south of Reading. The early history of Spencers Wood so far as we can recover it is the story of that common. And it must be suggested that, in some loose way, the common recorded by Rocque was where the wood with which Blunt was familiar stood. We have to assume that it was, at some time, felled, and that the use of the common for grazing prevented any regeneration. (We can guess that the wood covered a larger area than the common, as will be explained.) What Spencers Wood meant to people in the eighteenth and early nineteenth centuries was an open space which the road to Basingstoke traversed after Three Mile Cross. It is noteworthy that Ordnance Survey maps in the later nineteenth century still refer to Spencers Wood as 'Spencerswood Common' although, by that time, the common had been enclosed. But even a common has a history. And a common can leave its mark on the present.

The history of Spencers Wood common is complicated by the peculiar feudal geography of this district. You may be familiar with the idea of the manor. Generally in lowland England a manor was the lands of a lord based on, and surrounding, a village. The boundaries of a manor encompassed the village and its fields and commons: they were often the same as the boundary of the parish. This sort of arrangement is conspicuously lacking south of Reading. There is a parish of Shinfield and there is a manor of Shinfield, but the parish of Shinfield also contained a number of other manors whose names will mean little to people today: Diddenham, Hartley Dummer, Moor Place, Little Shipridge with Garstons, and Bealmes.[2] It seems likely that this reflects the medieval colonisation of the area and its clearance from woodland. The smaller manors were probably grants of woods – assarts – which never developed into manors as they would normally be understood. The signs are that they were centred around moated manorial centres such as survive at Bealmes and Sheepbridge Court; they had only small numbers of tenants and never evolved either villages or open fields. But they had commons, and a common implies commoners who had the right to use the common, and in turn that implies a bounded area within which the holders of land were entitled to use the common. Normally it is a case that every manor had its own common, but commons can run over the boundaries of manors, allowing the free passage of animals from one manor to the next (as proves to be the case with Spencers Wood common).

Spencers Wood though is brimful with complications. The area from Three Mile Cross to the county boundary beyond Riseley, and including Swallowfield, was until 1844 in Wiltshire and not Berkshire, as shown on the map on p. 6. Spencers Wood common was divided between two parishes – Shinfield and Swallowfield – and three manors, Shinfield, Little Shipridge with Garstons, and Bealmes. As a result it took three enclosure awards to enclose the common. Not even its end is straightforward.

The medieval history of this area remains to be fully worked out, and probably never will be. Much of the requisite knowledge had already been lost by the eighteenth century. In 1733 the manorial jury of the manor of Little Shipridge with Garstons, one of the manors which concerns us here, could not declare the entire circuit of the manor's bounds and it is clear that by the time of the enclosure of the common 130 years later, knowledge of the feudal arrangements had atrophied even further. This essay is, then, a first attempt at recovering what has long been lost, some of it probably irretrievably. There is, though, a certain amount of material for us to exploit. There is a good map of the manor of Little Shipridge from as early as 1625 and splendid maps of Diddenham (to the west of Spencers Wood) of c.1760 and Shinfield (to the east) of 1756.[3] The Shinfield map shows the northern part of the common. The area that primarily concerns us, the manors of Bealmes and Little Shipridge with Garstons, probably never justified the expense of an eighteenth-century survey: certainly none survives. Instead, the full first map we have is Rocque's. Some forty years later there is a further map by Thomas Pride of the area around

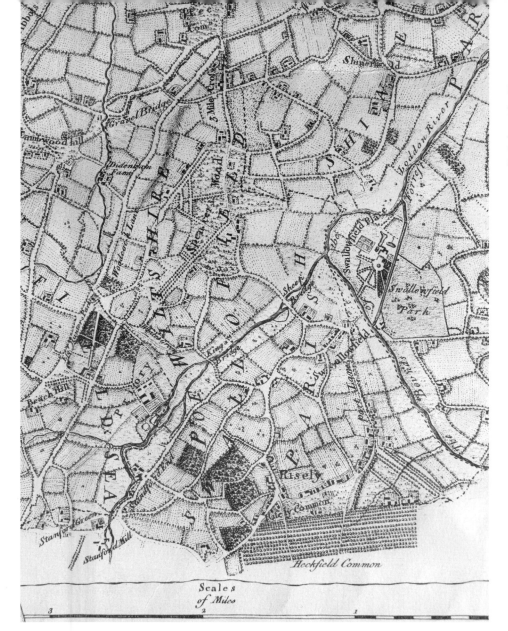

Extract from
John Roque, *A Topographical Survey of the County of Berks* (1761)

Reading and this shows additional detail – it is not, as is sometimes said, simply derivative of Rocque. It is with these two maps that we start.

Rocque's is an example of the late eighteenth-century genre of large-scale county maps. As freelance (and commercial) projects, these vary enormously in quality, but Rocque's map of Berkshire is one of the more superior efforts, showing minor roads and buildings, field boundaries, open fields and even the direction of ploughing within fields. As such it is a worthy predecessor of the Ordnance Survey (whose first large-scale mapping of Berkshire was surprisingly late). Spencers Wood common is one of a number of commons in the area: there are

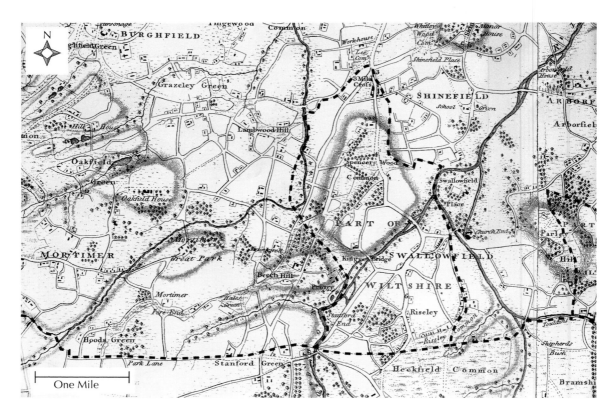

also smaller areas called greens, as in Shinfield Green, Ryeish Green and Whites Green (which forms the far end of Spencers Wood common near Kingsbridge) or the small Clares Green, little more than a wide road, which is marked towards the top right of the map opposite. Other than the commons and greens, Rocque portrayed a landscape which was largely enclosed: the road system, including the pattern of lanes between Spencers Wood and Shinfield is shown by him largely as it exists today. Where there was a substantial difference from the modern road pattern was that there was no Beech Hill Road until after the 1864 enclosure. This explains why Beech Hill Road is wide, straight – and fast.

Rocque shows the common as an area of rough grass and bushes and this plainly distinguishes it from the cultivated fields which surround it. It is easy enough to show the extent of the common on the 1872 map (opposite), which also shows the enclosure history of the common. It ought to be said that there is no reason to believe that the common shown in Rocque's map had the same extent as the common of 1660 or 1560: the likelihood is that it was undergoing a process of contraction as land was taken from it and put under cultivation. The common is merely a residual: what is left at any given time after what was judged worth enclosing had been enclosed. If one looks at the map, the

Extract from Thomas Pride, *A topographical map of the town of Reading and the country adjacent…* (1790), highlighting the county boundaries, including the detached parts of Wiltshire

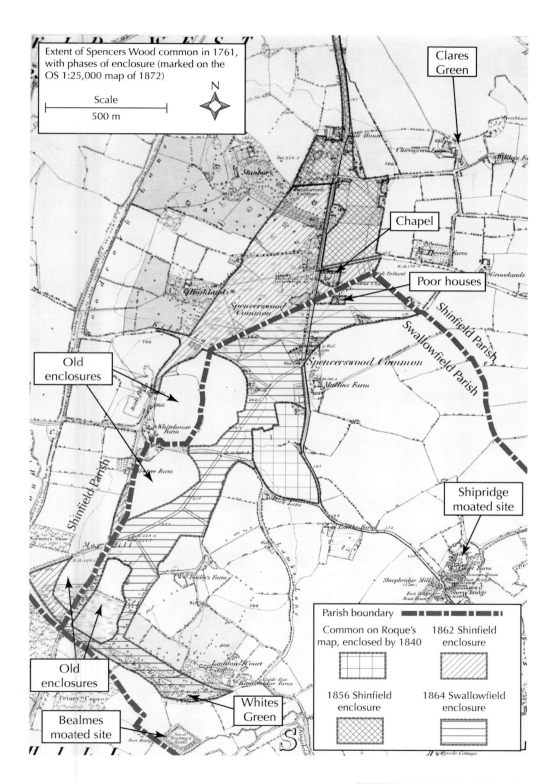

Extent of Spencers Wood common in 1761, with phases of enclosure (marked on the OS 1:25,000 map of 1872)

Scale
500 m

N

Clares Green

Chapel

Poor houses

Shinfield Parish

Swallowfield Parish

Old enclosures

Shipridge moated site

Old enclosures

Whites Green

Bealmes moated site

Parish boundary

Common on Roque's map, enclosed by 1840

1862 Shinfield enclosure

1856 Shinfield enclosure

1864 Swallowfield enclosure

two oval enclosures to the east of Whitehouse Farm and Yew Tree Farm are plainly enclosed from the common. The process of enclosure appears to have continued even after Rocque made his survey: the southern part of the area shown as common had been converted into fields by the nineteenth century. Apart from this, though, the area shown by Rocque is the area enclosed in the mid-nineteenth century.

The common was also being nibbled away by the enclosure of areas within it. Several encroachments are shown on Rocque's map: in the maps opposite we show how they developed using the Shinfield estate plan (1756), the tithe map (1838) and two nineteenth-century Ordnance Survey plans (1872, 1899). There was an enclosure – A – containing a house by the side of the road midway between (in modern terms) The Square and Clares Green Road. This enclosure was plainly shown as hedged on the 1756 Shinfield map. By the time of the 1838 tithe map it contained several houses, including two (numbered 516 and 518) that appear to be semi-detached. Parcel 519 was described as a blacksmith's shop at the time of the tithe map. The house numbered 520 and the two detached houses were still shown on the Ordnance Survey of 1872 but by 1899 the site had been cleared and a much larger house, with gardens, had been built to the north. The lower part of the site was progressively built over with houses facing onto the Basingstoke Road, but the boundary of the encroachment remains the property boundary at the rear of some of them. These properties all belonged to H. L. Hunter of Beech Hill House at the time of the tithe map and it can be shown that the original encroachment was leased to one Whiting in 1729. When this lease fell in, the cottages were rack-rented, the largest to one John Wheatley for £8. The enclosure was also enlarged by other small encroachments made in 1817.[4]

On the east side of the common, there were common-edge enclosures for cottages, two of which were shown on the Shinfield map. The first – B – is a tear-shaped enclosure which is at the rear of what became the site for St Michael's Church. By the time of the tithe map, it had been subdivided into at least five cottages numbered 371–76, but the first edition Ordnance Survey map shows that most of them had been cleared away by 1872. The upper part of the enclosure was finally incorporated into the gardens of the houses on Basingstoke Road, but some of the line of its western boundary just about survives as a property boundary. At the time of the tithe map, these cottages belonged to A. C. Cobham, the lord of the manor of Shinfield.

A further enclosure is shown on the Shinfield map on the eastern edge of the common – C. By the time of the tithe map a second enclosure had been made nearby and there were two cottages numbered 498 and 499, both with small gardens. These cottages were Hunter's property. After enclosure a short,

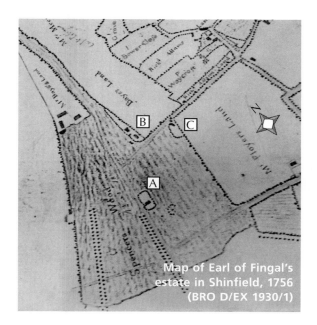

Map of Earl of Fingal's estate in Shinfield, 1756 (BRO D/EX 1930/1)

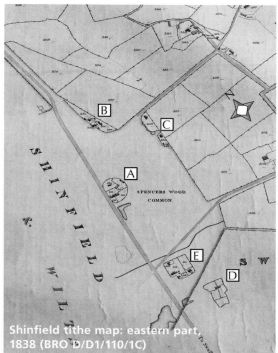

Shinfield tithe map: eastern part, 1838 (BRO D/D1/110/1C)

The development of encroachments on Spencers Wood common before and after enclosure. Letters A, B, C, D and E are referred to in the text

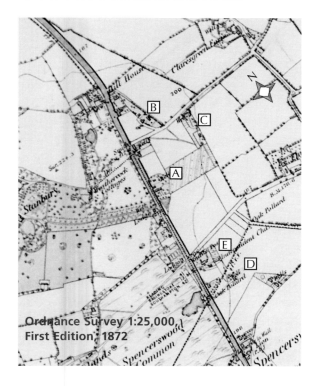

Ordnance Survey 1:25,000, First Edition, 1872

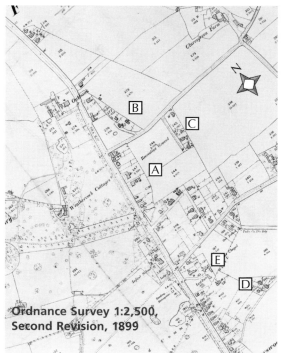

Ordnance Survey 1:2,500, Second Revision, 1899

dead-end road was made to give access to the houses: this survives as Recreation Lane which leads off Clares Green Road, but the cottages themselves have long gone and been replaced by modern houses.

Further south Rocque shows an enclosure set back from the road and roughly on the site of Spring Gardens – D . These were the poor cottages for Swallowfield. They were leased to the parish for 99 years by the lord of the manor of Little Shipridge with Garstons, Rev. James Phipps, in 1733, and then leased for a further 99 years by the then lord, H. L. Hunter, in 1837. The use of commons as space on which to build cottages for the poor (or workhouses, as at Lea common) is not unusual and was sanctioned in the Old Poor Law of 1601;[5] but these were cottages for Swallowfield parish, built within a matter of yards of the parish boundary. Given their location, one wonders whether they originated as pest cottages (cottages to isolate people infected with the plague) in the previous century, but this is surmise. The cottages had a garden: their extent is conveniently shown on a plan inset into the 1837 lease.[6]

A final encroachment on the common which ought to be mentioned here came long after Rocque's map but again shows the use of commons for public purposes. This was the grant of an enclosure – E – on the common for use as a non-conformist Sunday School and church room, made in 1816.[7] As is explained in Chapter Five, the building erected then survived into the twentieth century when it was superseded by the Congregational Church (now made into private houses) by the roadside: the original Sunday School and church building lay some distance back from the road. The tithe map shows the chapel (512) and its garden (511), but by this time there were two other cottages (513 and 514) and a larger dwelling house with garden (515). Whether these houses predated the chapel, or followed on it, cannot be ascertained at the moment.

Rocque's map also shows three buildings in the angle between Beech Hill Road and Basingstoke Road (by the foot of the 'I' of 'Swallofield' [sic]). These must be the leasehold cottages, noted in a rental of the Hunter estate in 1828 as standing opposite Body's Farm: they had gone by the time the tithe map was made.[8]

Otherwise Rocque's map, and at a later date Pride's, show the classic pattern of common-side settlement. This is where houses are built on the edge of the common, on the common-side and looking out onto the common. (There is a splendid example of this shown on Rocque's map at Riseley common.) The north end of the common was marked by Hill House. There are then three sets of cottages on the western side of the common: Weathercock Cottage (now demolished), then what may be the modern Highlands Cottage, and then a third set of buildings also demolished. Buildings are also shown on the site of

Body's Farm: this too should be counted as a common-side settlement. By the time of the tithe map a further encroachment had appeared along Kiln Lane. One of the buildings erected here survives as Oak Tree Cottage, described in *Our Village of Spencers Wood* (2001).[9]

Exceptionally, we have a description of the common written by Mary Russell Mitford (1787–1855), the lady novelist of Three Mile Cross.

> Turning again up the hill [from Three Mile Cross], we find ourselves on that peculiar charm of English scenery, a green common, divided by the road; the right [west] side fringed by hedgerows and trees, with cottages and farmhouses irregularly placed, and terminated by a double avenue of noble oaks; the left [east side], prettier still, dappled by bright pools of water and islands of cottages and cottage gardens and sinking gradually down to corn fields and meadows and an old farmhouse ... The common is itself the prettiest part of the prospect; half covered with low furze, whose golden blossoms reflect so intensely the last beams of the setting sun, and alive with cows and sheep and two sets of cricketers.[10]

This seems a fairly exact description of what she would have seen from the crest of the hill. Elsewhere she describes the pond on the common being used for skating in winter.[11]

This is probably an extremely rose-tinted view of the common. Less romantic eyes would have seen it as an area of poor-quality grassland, probably with gorse (used as fuel) and, by 1850, a few standard trees.[12] The extant court rolls say nothing very much about the management of the common: one would guess, but no more than that, that it was heavily grazed in an uncontrolled fashion and for that reason was of little agricultural utility. The little direct evidence we have on this comes from the years immediately before enclosure. In a letter of 1849, written by the lord of the manor, H. L. Hunter, to his steward at a time when he was contemplating holding a manorial court, Hunter reflected that Spencers Wood common was 'a good deal abused by people turning out sheep etc who have no right'. This was the fault, he thought of the Hayward: he therefore proposed dismissing the Hayward in post and appointing one of his tenants who lived near the common and who, one supposes, would keep it under closer supervision.[13] (A Hayward was a manorial officer responsible for ensuring that hedges and fences were kept in order, but here he was also responsible for supervising the common.) The Inclosure Commissioners, commenting on the common on the eve of its enclosure in 1861, said that 'Inclosure will put an end to trespassing and enable the land to be converted to profitable uses' and 'Inclosure will put an end to the illegal stocking of the land, and largely increase its value'.[14] Of course, one person's illegal stocking is another person's livelihood.

The court rolls show that haywards had been appointed from time to time by the manorial court. But courts were only held very intermittently (perhaps only as much as once a decade after 1750) and the court rolls contain no prosecutions for overgrazing or illegal grazing.[15] The eighteenth-century ones do contain formulaic injunctions against the improper use of the common – the removal of turf etc, but without a court to punish malefactors, it seems unlikely that even the most enthusiastic hayward could do anything to manage the common.

In one respect though the common was a managed space. Rocque shows what are plainly avenues of trees – elms or oaks – crossing the common and flanking it on its west side. A long avenue is also shown extending from the common along the line of Beech Hill Road. A similar pattern is shown by Pride. The 1756 Shinfield map shows two avenues, one adjacent to the road and the other parallel to the western boundary of the common, in the northern part of the common belonging to Shinfield manor. A map of two fields and two cottages on Lambs Lane made in 1809 plainly shows the avenue stretching down the line of the modern Beech Hill Road.[16] Mary Russell Mitford mentions them in the quotation from *Our Village* (p. 11 above): elsewhere she refers to 'the open common with its park-like trees' and the 'straight and regular double avenue of oaks nearly a mile long' which ran along the line of Beech Hill Road.[17]

So the common had been deliberately and carefully planted with long avenues at some point in the eighteenth century: from the map, it looks like a conventional parkland landscape of the earlier part of the century. But who was responsible can only be guessed at. We have a letter from Joseph Danvers to the first H. L. Hunter of April 1742 when negotiations were advanced for Hunter's purchase of the manor of Bealmes. Hunter had evidently queried aspects of the particulars describing the manor that he had been sent. Danvers was anxious to justify what had been written: 'If I lived in the country I could raise that estate considerably by enclosing some of the waste ground without prejudice to the commons and by planting the commons as other neighbouring manors have done but living at a distance I have not done it yet'. We have a particular of the manor – unfortunately undated, but one assumes it was the one that Hunter had before him – which comments how 'The commons are extensive and improvable with a considerable quantity of young trees, 4,000 planted'. A later Hunter thought that his grandfather, the purchaser of 1742, had planted the avenues on the commons. So we are left supposing that one or other successive lords of the manor planted the avenues in the second quarter of the eighteenth century.[18] Certainly the trees on the common belonged to the lord of the manor. The manorial survey of 1733 unfortunately makes no mention of the lord's right to trees either on tenements or on the common, but an advert for 368 oak trees available to fell on the estates of Henry Hunter, and placed in the *Reading Mercury* of 1776, includes five oaks standing on Spencers Wood common.

It seems likely that the avenues were felled in the early nineteenth century. In about 1851, George Haydon, Hunter's retired bailiff, made a deposition to prove Hunter's right to the common. The deposition refers to some of the avenue being felled around 1810; the oaks felled at that time were on the western side of the road near Hill House and arranged in three rows. Other trees were felled about 1820.[19] An advertisement in the *Berkshire Chronicle* in 1839 offered for sale oak trees standing in the 'Avenue' on Spencers Wood common and at other locations.[20] By the time the tithe maps were made, they had all gone. (In general the district was more wooded then than now: in 1855 119 oak trees and 163 elm trees were offered for sale on Hill House Farm.[21])

Another feature of the common was its ponds, of which only one or two survive. Four are noted on the first edition Ordnance Survey: one just south of Hill House; a second just south of Weathercock Farm (later cottage), which has now been filled in, a third on the east side of Basingstoke Road, also now filled in, on the site of Birch Court, and the fourth the familiar Spencers Wood pond. The question is whether these ponds should be seen as natural features or whether they are man-made excavations. The evidence points to the latter. In 1763 the court of the manor of Bealmes complained that the surveyor of the Reading to Basingstoke road had been digging pits for road gravel, one of which was expressly said to be on the common. He was instructed to make them safe.[22] Some of the other ponds may have been made to give cattle water to drink: the water table is high but there is a lack of water on the common (although the earlier maps show a rather desultory stream, now disappeared, flowing east-west over the common).

*     *     *

As we said earlier, this area was divided between a number of small manors, knowledge of which had largely been lost even by the early nineteenth century. When a perambulation was made of the manor of Little Shipridge with Garstons in 1733, the tenants making the perambulation admitted that they did not know the full bounds of the manor: the perambulation peters out. We have a much earlier perambulation of the manor of Bealmes made in 1686. In 1745 the manorial court confirmed the perambulation made sixty years before: but by its nature, and its reliance on lost place names, houses and lands belonging to long-dead landowners, and tenants and landmarks (especially trees) long since removed, it is hard to relate to the landscape.[23] At some later date, probably in 1810,[24] a perambulation was held over two days during which a large body of locals pushed their way through hedges and crossed gardens and at the end of the first day were entertained with 18 gallons of beer at the Bound Tree (the boundary tree) at Whites Green. Even if the bounds were not memorable, the hangover doubtless was. There are multiple difficulties with this perambulation: two manors were merged into one: the route they took was plainly nonsense and the clerk who was charged with writing up the perambulation, perhaps realising that futility of the project, gave up part way through. It peters out into a few pencil notes, and then stops on the road to Farley Hill.[25] It is clear that, although the manorial courts of Bealmes and of Little Shipridge with Garstons were still occasionally held in the nineteenth century, knowledge of their boundaries had been lost. Hence there were occasional conflicts over boundaries, including a spat over the felling of timber trees on Hyde End Green, and when the manor of Shinfield was perambulated, Hunter had his bailiff meet the Shinfield party on the common and object to the boundary they claimed.[26]

When it came to enclosure, the identity of the manors in which the common lay was a question of some importance, for the rights of the lord of the manor (the notional owners of the soil) had to be compensated. The north and eastern part of the common (shown on the map on p. 7), was held to belong to the manor of Shinfield and was enclosed in 1856. But the north-west and middle part of the common was held to belong to the manor of Little Shipridge with Garstons. The Shinfield map of 1756 (see p. 9) shows the whole of this area as belonging to Shinfield manor. On enclosure, the southern part of the common, with the long extension down to Whites Green, was deemed to belong to the manor of Swallowfield, but this was a straightforward error. The manor of Swallowfield, so far as it can be discovered, did not extend even as far west as the modern village of Swallowfield (which was in the manor of Bealmes).[27] The 'Swallowfield' enclosure, completed in 1864, besides tidying up small areas here and there, also enclosed Riseley common and Farley Hill common. It was perhaps this that led to confusion; it made sense to suppose that these commons fell in the area of the manor of Swallowfield because the manor of Bealmes had been all but forgotten. This mistake has important consequences, as we shall explain.

If it is not possible to establish the boundaries in great detail, it is possible to describe roughly the areas of the two manors from the perambulations. A map of the manor of Shipridge of 1625 shows that it covered the area to the east and west of Sheepbridge bridge and north of the river Loddon extending towards Spencers Wood. At some point the manor came to include the manor of Garstons. Garstons occurs as a field name to the east between Hyde End and the Loddon so it was possible that there was a further small manor here, the site of which is now lost. But the manor of Shipridge also included Trunkwell and here it is significant that the tithe map and first edition Ordnance Survey both show a detached part of Shinfield parish there, suggesting that the connection between Trunkwell and Shinfield is very old indeed. The implication is that the manor cannot have been contained within a continuous circuit.

The manor of Bealmes had an extraordinary shape: it too was probably not all contained within a single circuit. Basically it was the land to the south of the river Loddon between the river and the county boundary. It extended from Stanford End Bridge in the west to Jouldens at its south-east corner, and then to Swallowfield in the east. It also had a northwards extension which had Woodcock Lane on the west and Spencers Wood common on the east: this ran as far north as Three Mile Cross. The manor had a shape like a boot. There was then a detached part of the manor at Farley Hill which was also in a detached part of Wiltshire (see p. 6). In all, the manor had three commons: Spencers Wood in the north west, Riseley in the south and Farley Hill in the east.

The perambulations of 1686 (for Bealmes) and 1733 (for Little Shipridge with Garstons) suggest that Spencers Wood common was divided three ways by boundaries running diagonally over it from south west to north east. As we shall see, there is an argument to be made that the boundary between Shinfield manor and Little Shipridge with Garstons came down Clares Green Road and then continued along the same line over the common. What we can say with certainty is that the northern part belonged to Shinfield, the middle to Little Shipridge and the southern part to Bealmes. This explains why Spencers Wood common was enclosed by three enclosure awards, one for each manor, but the boundaries used were not those known historically.

The reason why the boundaries used on the enclosure maps were not the 'right' ones probably comes from the fact that, when the enclosure of the Shinfield part of the common was first proposed, A. C. Cobham, the lord of the manor of Shinfield, seems to have claimed the whole of the north of the common, from the parish boundary, as a part of his manor. This was no more and no less than what the Shinfield estate map of 1756 claimed. This was resisted by H. L. Hunter, the lord of Bealmes and of Little Shipridge with Garstons. Evidence was gathered on his behalf to prove his rights in the northern part of the common.[28] These included the planting and felling of trees but most crucially the licensing and taking of rent from the encroachments. Those lying to the south of Clares Green Road and a line drawn from it over the common were indisputably Hunter's and had a history extending back to c.1730: but those to the north were Cobham's. The conclusion was unavoidable: that the Hunters and their predecessors had exercised rights over the southern part of the area claimed by Cobham for Shinfield. Hence the peculiar boundaries of the 1856 and 1864 enclosures are probably a compromise between Cobham's exaggerated claim and Hunter's historical evidence.

The pattern of the boundaries of the common seem to be telling us something and, whilst what follows is speculation, it may be possible to verify this suggestion at a later date. The boundaries of the common are very straight. In landscape terms, straight lines in the landscape often indicate planning and the calculated division of land by surveyors, in short, an act of formal enclosure over an extensive area. Curved lines, on the other hand, suggest incremental enclosure over long periods, a progressive enclosure undertaken by many hands. (This often called assarting.) The western boundaries of the common are essentially straight, and, when one stands back from the map, there is an area to the east of the common where the layout of roads (Clares Green Road, Hyde End Road etc) is notably rectilinear and the roads themselves form something of a grid. On the other hand, there is the shape of Hyde End Lane, with its gentle curve which suggests that it was running round the edge of something, and that something may have been the wood called Spencers Wood. And so we arrive at a suggestion. The wood lay between Hyde End Lane on the east and Woodcock Lane on the west (see the map on p. vi). It was shared between the surrounding manors. At some point it was enclosed by an agreement between the lords of Shinfield, Little Shipridge with Garstons, and Bealmes and partitioned between them, which is why Bealmes in particular has such strange boundaries. Part of the wood was reserved as a common: the remainder was laid out on a sub-rectangular grid. The wood itself was felled. It needs to be stressed that at the moment there is no *documentary* proof for this suggestion, but it is a scenario in accordance with the record of the landscape.

\*   \*   \*

Having explained why there were three enclosure awards, it is harder to explain why there was most of a decade between the first award, enclosing the northern end of the common, and the second and third, enclosing the southern end.[29] The first Shinfield enclosure was commenced in 1845 but not completed until 1856. The Inclosure Commissioners published notices of their intention to bring forwards proposals for the enclosure of the remainder of Spencers Wood common in the *Berkshire Chronicle* on 19 January 1861.

By this date enclosure was no longer undertaken by the authority of individual private acts and enclosure commissioners but under the sanction of a General Enclosure Act passed in 1845.[30] The Inclosure Commissioners appointed local agents to act as commissioners, value the lands and make the actual allocations: these were approved by the commissioners and given parliamentary sanction by an annual act approving the commissioners' work. By this date the main enclosure movement had run its course and much of the work of the commissioners can be seen as a tidying of overlooked areas. A glance at the enclosure maps for Shinfield and Swallowfield shows how much of the land remaining to be enclosed was actually small greens, or wide grass verges (driftways). But enclosure was also a more thorough reorganisation of the landscape, especially the creation and closure of roads and field paths. It was, in more senses than one, a privatisation of the landscape, a process whereby people were excluded from areas that they had been accustomed to use, whether in their daily business or for recreation.

The enclosure of a common abolished the common rights of grazing (and any other rights exercised over it, like collecting fuel) and turned an open, collectively owned space into parcels in private ownership. The underlying principle was that after the lord of the manor had been compensated for his manorial rights by giving him a share of the land, the commoners were compensated for their right to graze the lands by sharing amongst them the remainder of the area of the common. This necessarily involved an investigation into who had the right to graze the common and the challenging of some whose rights were spurious or were based on recent usage alone. It seems that in the case of Spencers Wood, the landowners of the *parishes* rather than the landowners within the *manors* were held to be the commoners. The result was that large numbers of individuals, including people who owned a house and little more, were given the right to a share of the commons. As the allocation of the common was made by *value*, people with little land but a house with a high rateable value received disproportionately more than people who were simply landowners.

Whilst the process was a public one, with every stage advertised and the appropriate documents made available for scrutiny, it was really a closed negotiation between the landowners and the valuer appointed by them who undertook the enclosure. The first meeting, convened at the Swan Inn in Three Mile Cross on 2 September 1861 to appoint the valuer, was attended by only seven people, including F. W. Allfrey of Stanbury and William Merry of Highlands. H. L. Hunter of Beech Hill House took the chair.[31]

The second Shinfield award allocated an area of 56½ acres but the claims on it came from 440 acres with common rights. Of the 'commoners', eight had less than one acre in land but three owned a total of 336½ acres. When it comes to the land awarded to the commoners, only three were awarded more than five acres. Seven were awarded less than a quarter acre and 13 less than an acre. The larger landowners were awarded about eight per cent of their landed area: so William Merry of Highlands with 50 acres received six acres; F. W. Allfrey with 138 received 10½; H. L. Hunter with 147 acres received a little under 20 acres, some of which he immediately sold on. (His allotment in compensation for his rights as lord were separate to this.)

In the Swallowfield award, the allotted area was 194.4 acres, but almost exactly ten times this area had claims to commonable rights. Eighteen 'commoners' had less than an acre: six had more than 100 acres, fifteen more than ten acres. As a result, people with ten acres or more of land were allocated around 7 or 8 per cent of the enclosed ground they held in the parish. So, the Duke of Wellington owned 205 acres and received 16 acres on enclosure. H. L. Hunter of Beech Hill had 342.5 acres of land and received 34.5 acres. Again, people owning house property were allocated proportionately more because of the value of their property: they generally received a quarter or a fifth of the area of their property.

The allocation of land on the enclosure of the commons reflected the ownership of the land which claimed common rights and so a small number of people received the lion's share of the land of the former commons and a much larger number received allotments which were no larger than house plots. These were placed along the Basingstoke Road, an invitation for development to start. And this, of course, is why the enclosure was so important. The justification for enclosure was the improvement of the land, but much of the land left to be enclosed by this late date was, by its nature, of limited potential: that is why it had not been enclosed earlier. Given the number of claimants, the limited area available and the costs of enclosure and improvement, it has to be questioned whether the larger landowners were enthusiastic about the whole process: there was relatively little advantage in it for them. But enclosing the common made it available for reshaping, either for the new landscape that F. W. Allfrey was to create at Stanbury, or more ordinarily, for building. Without the enclosure, Spencers Wood could not have developed in the way that it did. It was not easy to build on a common with any assurance: the common needed to be enclosed to release the lands for sale.

The first enclosure award was relatively generous in its provision of public space. In Spencers Wood, a strange arrangement was arrived at where a parcel of three acres – numbered 52 on the enclosure plan and now the Spencers Wood Recreation Ground – was allocated to the lord of the manor of Shinfield on the condition that he preserved its surface (i.e. did not plough it) and grazed only sheep on it: it was to be made available for the exercise and recreation of the inhabitants. The next field down, 54 on the enclosure plan, also of three acres, was given as an allotment for the use of the 'labouring poor'. This parcel was being used as (garden) allotments as early as 1879, and its use in this way may go back further, perhaps to the moment of enclosure itself.[32]

In 1861, explaining why it was not proposed to make any provision for allotments or recreation grounds in the Shinfield enclosure then under way, the Inclosure Commissioners held that adequate provision had already been made by the first Shinfield award and no more was needed. Addressing the enclosure of the commons of Swallowfield (Bealmes) manor, they argued that the cottages already had gardens attached.[33] The second Shinfield award made no allocation of public space, but the Swallowfield (Bealmes) enclosure allocated four acres in Riseley village for recreation.

The awards did though make an odd concession to public need by making two of the existing ponds into public ponds. The 1856 Shinfield award provided for a public pond on the east side of the Basingstoke Road – now disappeared under houses. The 1863 award made the familiar Spencers Wood pond into a public pond to be maintained by a rate levied on the area enclosed by the award. The ground immediately to the north was to be made into a public quarry – or rather a gravel pit – for the maintenance of the roads. In time this might have developed into a second pond.

It might be asked whether this took place without any public comment. In fact there is nothing to be found on the enclosure in the Reading papers: no letters, no reports of protest or other meetings, no editorial musings about the desirability or otherwise of the enclosure, nothing that gives us a clue as to how people felt about the enclosure. The failure to articulate objections should not be taken to indicate willing acceptance. We lack any correspondence with the Inclosure Commission's valuer undertaking the enclosure which might show what pressure he was placed under and how the enclosure was shaped by landlord and public opinion, but whether all voices would treated as equal is doubtful. Had Spencers Wood common survived for a further twenty years, then it might never have been enclosed. (The two enclosure awards of 1863 and 1864 were the last to be made in Berkshire.) By the late 1860s attitudes to enclosure were beginning to turn. The remaining open ground came to be valued not as an unexploited opportunity for agricultural improvement or property development but for its value as an open space for recreation. If the common had remained unenclosed, then it might have had a second life as a park fringed with villas looking over it: but it was perhaps too far from Reading to be attractive to the commercial middle classes. As it is, if one looks around, then one is aware that many of the late nineteenth- and early twentieth-century developments took place on former commons where, because of the process of enclosure, landownership was splintered, and the quality of the ground made agriculture a hopeless prospect.

For those who look, the common has left its mark on Spencers Wood. The view towards Highlands over what is colloquially but incorrectly called 'The Common' gives a sense of what that landscape might have looked like 200 years ago. The rather rampant gorse bush by the Post Office bus stop is surely the lineal descendant of many others that covered the pre-enclosure common. The boundaries of the common, and the boundaries of many of the allotments made at the enclosure, are in many cases still property boundaries.

It is easy to assume that the history of Spencers Wood starts with the enclosure of the common, but as we hope to have shown here, there is a history (or perhaps we should say a prehistory) before enclosure. This is a first essay about a part of a larger landscape, indeed as an essay about a common, about the edges and margins of that landscape. There is much more to be done, and in time it might even be possible to say with certainty what happened to the wood, and where it was, and so make a clean sweep of the questions with which we started.

## Notes

[1] Berkshire Record Office (hereafter BRO), R/Z1/1.

[2] There wasn't even agreement over how to spell Shipridge. I use 'Sheepbridge' as the modern name, but historically the spelling is Shepridge, or Shipridge, which I use when referring to the manor. Bealmes is also spelt Beames or Beamys.

[3] Respectively D/EB P4; D/EBY/P14; D/EX 1930/1. The survey accompanying the Shinfield map is D/ESa E3. I am grateful to Barry Boulton for drawing this to my attention.

[4] These details are taken from one of the key documents, a collection of evidence collected in 1851 to prove the rights of H. L. Hunter in the common: D/EBb O3/13 (unlisted bundle), 'Ex Parte H. L. Hunter, 1851'.

[5] Sara Birtles, 'Common lands, poor relief and enclosure: the use of manorial resources in fulfilling parish obligations, 1601–1834', Past and Present 165 (1999), pp. 74–106.

[6] BRO, D/EHR/T44 1-2.

[7] BRO, D/N 44/6/2/1/1 (memorandum about the founding of the chapel, 1826).

[8] BRO, EBB M2 (unfoliated).

[9] Parcels 560–62 on the tithe map.

[10] Mary Russell Mitford, Our Village (1893 edn), p. 23. Furze is gorse.

[11] Ibid., p. 29.

[12] Mitford refers to the cottages burning turf: ibid., p. 29.

[13] EBB M/3, letter, Hunter to Blandy, 12 Oct 1849. The same bundle contains a paper gathering together references to the Hayward from the court rolls.

[14] British Parliamentary Papers, 1861 XX (833), Inclosure Commission, Special report of the commissioners, 1861, p. 4.

[15] The Bealmes court was held only nine times between 1750 and 1800 and five times in the nineteenth century, the last time in 1858: D/EHR M56. That for Little Shipridge and Garstons was normally held at the same time.

[16] BRO, D/EZ 10.

[17] Mitford, Our village, pp. 49, 33.

[18] D/EHR E4/12, letter, Danvers to Hunter, 26 April 1742; M62 (unnumbered bundle: there are two slightly different copies of the particulars in this bundle); D/Ebb O3/13, 'Ex parte H. L. Hunter, 1851', recollections of George Haydon.

[19] D/Ebb O3/13, 'Ex parte H. L. Hunter, 1851'.

[20] Berkshire Chronicle, 23, 30 Mar. 1839.

[21] Berkshire Chronicle, 28 Apr. 1855.

[22] D/EHR/M43 (unlisted listed bundle, presentments, 21 Nov. 1763).

[23] For Little Shipridge and Garston, see D/EBB/M1, court held 3 Oct. 1733; for Bealmes we have used a copy of the perambulation in EBb/M3.

[24] D/EBb O3/13, 'Ex parte H. L. Hunter, 1851' contains an account of the perambulation.

[25] BRO, EBb M3 (unlisted bundle).

[26] D/EBb O3/13, 'Ex parte H. L. Hunter, 1851', recollections of George Haydon.

[27] For what may be the extent of the manor of Swallowfield, see the enclosure map of 1817 on the Berkshire Record Office's 'New Landscapes' Web site, www.berkshireenclosure.org.uk/.

[28] BRO, D/EBb O3/13, 'Ex parte H. L. Hunter, 1851'.

[29] The awards and their supporting maps are all available on the 'New Landscapes' Web site. The dates given are those on the awards themselves, not the date when they formally passed into law.

[30] For a helpful study of late enclosure, Alun Howkins, 'The use and abuse of English commons, 1845–1914', History Workshop Journal 78 (2014), pp. 107–32.

[31] D/EBb O3/13, minutes and draft minutes of the meeting.

[32] BRO, D/EX 303 E1/8 Shinfield, Floyers Farm (45a) … with plan.

[33] Inclosure Commissioners, Special report 1861, p. 4.

# CHAPTER TWO

# The Natural Environment

*Patricia Green*

Today, Spencers Wood is still a distinct village within its own countryside setting. The natural environment of fields, ponds, hedges and woods surrounds the roads and properties, and people can see and walk into this countryside from their homes. Despite the massive development that is scheduled to take place during the next ten or so years, the environment will remain a part of and an influence on the community. 'The outdoors' provides a sense of place, and a background to local actions and activities, and the feeling you get as you drive through the village is one of 'leafiness'.

The landscape of Spencers Wood is a gentle farmed scene of fields and small woods, with meadows and hedgerows that are important for wildlife. The land rises gradually from the Loddon valley in the south to hills on the west and north of the village that fall away abruptly down to the valleys of the Kennet and Thames. From these hills there are views over fields and trees to the south, wide views along the Kennet valley to the west, and views over Reading and the Thames directly to the Chiltern Hills in the north. To the east, farmland gives way to the houses of Shinfield village. The underlying geology is London clay which breaks down at the surface to form the thick, poorly draining soil typical of much of Spencers Wood. On the hills the clay is capped by the plateau gravels deposited during the Ice Age. These gravels allow water to percolate through to the clay, where it moves horizontally to come out at the surface in lines of springs and ponds. Soils on the gravels are generally easier to work and warmer than the clay soils. Fields beside the River Loddon have a covering of fertile alluvium, but are frequently very wet.

The resulting landscape is one of fields used for grazing and for growing crops, with woodland remaining on the steeper slopes west of the village. There are scattered copses often around ponds in the fields and beside the roads. The *Landscape Character Assessment* produced by Wokingham District (now Wokingham Borough) Council describes the wetland area of the Loddon River Valley as one of high-quality landscape due to its braided course and the absence of development. Many small streams and ditches flow from the south

side of Hyde End Road and from the west of Basingstoke Road down to the river and there are clusters of ancient willow trees along its bank.

The same document describes the clay farmlands and built-up areas of Spencers Wood as a landscape of 'overall moderate quality', citing the variety of field sizes with their mix of pasture and grazing land, and the important interlinked hedgerows with significant mature trees, which are a major feature along Basingstoke Road. The many blocks of woodland and copses especially along the hilltop above the Common are other major defining features. The document mentions fields reserved for horse keeping, such as those off Basingstoke Road and Ryeish Lane. This is typical of areas at the edge of denser settlement where horse riding provides a better return from the land than does

Tree-lined Basingstoke Road, looking north in the early twentieth century, past the Infants' School (*opposite*); looking south from the same point in 2015 (*right*)

Farmland wrapping around the village (*opposite below*) Meadows and hedgerows are important for wildlife (*below*)

traditional farming. The open spaces of the 'Common' and the adjacent open parklands around Stanbury and Highlands are other distinctive characteristics of the village environment.

There are still some fields that have never been intensively farmed, where the absence of fertilisers and other chemicals has allowed native wild flowers to remain. Such unimproved grasslands usually have characteristic anthills with their customary small early spring flowering plants that attract a range of insects. The 'Common', which is informally open for public access has a good range of wild plants that flower in due season, and there are a few fields west of Sevenoaks Drive and one near the end of White House Lane which are very rich in wild flowers. The fields north of Clares Green Road have a variety of

Ponds on clay soils beside lanes: one example at a corner of Ryeish Lane

Footpath through woods above the 'Common'

Parkland of
meadows
and scattered
trees, from the
gateway to
Highlands

Wetlands with
willows

Stile leading to the 'Common', and the public footpath across to the woodland

Scattered mature trees and flower-rich grass of the 'Common' (*opposite top*)

Cattle grazing in the Clares Green SANG (*opposite*)

wildflowers and form an area of valuable biodiversity as they link with the surrounding hedgerows and the adjacent pond. This area is open for access to everyone and it was recognised to be a valuable part of the environment in its early designation as a Local Wildlife Site.

In 2014 this designation was changed to a Suitable Alternative Natural Greenspace (SANG). SANGs are natural areas open to the public for walking and informal recreation, as directed by the European Union to guide people away from walking (especially with dogs) over land that is used by ground-nesting birds which are declining and endangered species – in this case particularly the nightjars that nest at Bramshill. There will be several SANGs around the edges of proposed development on the east of Spencers Wood but most are on intensively farmed land and will have limited wildlife value for many decades. The one with the most interesting biodiversity will be the Loddon SANG, which is just outside the Spencers Wood area. The Clares Green SANG is managed partly by mowing and partly by grazing by small herds of cattle brought in for a set time, see the photograph opposite. Only docile, unfussy breeds of cattle that tolerate the public and their dogs well are chosen for this task.

Many fields to the east of Basingstoke Road were used as orchards when this area supplied the markets of Reading, and although most are now developed or about to be built upon, remnant fruit trees grow in many gardens and on 'left over' land, like the plum trees outside Spring Gardens.

The trees of Spencers Wood are important to the environment. There are several species of interesting planted trees, noticeably Scots pines and sugar maples along Basingstoke Road, but among the evergreen trees that provide a green outlook in the winter months, it is the Sequoias along Wellington Court that stand out as the iconic trees of the village. The hilltop avenue of these large trees can be seen from across the Kennet valley and it serves as a landmark from junction 11 of the M4. This type of tree had been named 'Wellingtonia' to commemorate the Duke of Wellington, and many were also planted in the grounds of Highlands and Stanbury. Although the Wellingtonias are not native trees, they provide shelter, nesting and feeding sites for birds such as nuthatches and tree creepers, and hosts of insects appreciate their soft-fissured bark. The avenue is within an older avenue of veteran oak trees and together they form a significant wildlife corridor link between the fields to the west and the

Spencers Wood pond, from the main road (*top*) in the early twentieth century and (*above*) completely overgrown in 2015, with sign for Chandler's Unisex Hair Salon

hedgerows along Basingstoke Road. Oak trees support more species of insects than any other trees in Britain, and are hosts to many birds.

English oaks are the majority species of tree in Spencers Wood, and there are veteran trees with girths of about three metres and an estimated age of between two and three hundred years. The area was an outlying part of the royal hunting forest of Windsor, so some trees may be descendants of those of pre-Norman times. Other frequently found trees are ash, willow and sycamore. Some trees line the roads and the river, but most are grouped on land that has been the least easy to farm or build upon. They are clustered around the ponds and wet depressions where gravel or clay has been extracted, for example, and around the pond on the 'Common', at the junction of Croft Road and Hyde End Lane, and at the back of houses south of Montgomery Drive.

Trees beside Lambs Lane form a substantial verge around a small stream. Trees and their understory shrubs and tall herb layer plants form complex habitats that support many creatures including birds and butterflies. One or two of the larger trees are used as night-time roosts by starlings.

The major area of trees is to the west of the 'Common', where the tree-lined hillsides are designated Local Wildlife Sites. This is mostly mixed ash woodland with oak, holly, and field maple. There is neglected hazel coppice, and some pine trees. The more open areas have ground flora with grasses. The thick clay soil has been used to make bricks and the remains of a kiln and loading bay can just be seen. The depressions left by the extraction of clay now fill with water most of the year. This adds to the complexity of wildlife habitats here, suiting dragonflies as a breeding location. A clear stream runs down the hillside to join the often waterlogged Woodcock Lane. Trees line the Lane, which is an ancient pathway, and it is lines of trees, hedgerows and footpaths that form the corridors for wildlife to move along and link with other communities, thus becoming more viable than if they were isolated.

The pond on the 'Common' is the largest body of open water in the village. The pond was cleaned and its margins reinstated during the winter of 2015–16, so that that area now receives more daylight and much less leaf fall. It is very attractive as a wildlife habitat, and is clearly visible from the main road and from the adjacent footpath.

The outlet passes under the road and is culverted thereafter. Fortunately many streams and ditches are open where they pass on verges beside the older roads, and they form valuable habitats especially when they are properly maintained. Amphibians, birds and insects are far more frequent and noticeable along these old lanes than in the newer developments, but where land is left with open water and some vegetation as at Benham Drive, there is the beginning of a new habitat for wildlife (see p. 43).

Spencers Wood pond from the 'Common' (*above*) in the early twentieth century and (*left*) after it was cleared in 2016

On clay lands the road surfaces are often lower than the surrounding fields, so the verges and ditches are useful in taking the water draining from the land. When the ditches become overgrown and blocked then the roads flood. This happens quite frequently along the spring line on the higher ground after heavy rainfalls, so the village can suffer flooding far away from the riverside.

Many footpaths around the village are another link to the natural world beyond the built environment. Woodcock Lane is one of the old routes, as is the path across the Common, with Mays Lane and Kiln Lane leading to the former brickworks. As the village becomes more developed, the links into the wider countryside will become increasingly important as corridor routes for wildlife.

The range of plants and open water habitats supports an interesting variety of fauna in the village. Bats (probably pipistrelle) are frequently seen during the late summer months, and other mammals include roe deer (which may not remain once the new developments proceed). There are woodpeckers and owls, and the red kites have successfully become local to the area. Smaller birds include long-tailed tits and goldfinches, with a

greater variety of birds coming into back gardens to feed during cold winters. Grouse and pheasants roam to feed over the fields, and they also visit gardens during hard weather. Rabbits and grey squirrels are often seen.

The attractive environment of Spencers Wood needs careful maintenance and protection if it is to retain its range of habitats and its value for wildlife. Wokingham Borough Council has produced a Biodiversity Action Plan (BAP) for its whole area, and it is hoped that Shinfield parish will draw up its own BAP. This will include an assessment of the local habitats of Spencers Wood and the variety of creatures here, with recommendations for works to safeguard and enhance them.

## Author's note

This chapter uses information from the *Landscape Character Assessment* (Wokingham Borough Council, 2004) and the *Biodiversity Action Plan for Wokingham District* (Wokingham Borough Council, 2003–12).

Hedgerows, which provide corridors of sanctuary for wildlife (*opposite top*); Woodcock Lane, an ancient route leading south into Hampshire (*opposite*); grass verges and garden trees, which enhance the environment (*above*); children enjoying the secluded narrow lanes, (*below*)

CHAPTER THREE

# The Development of the Village

*Patricia Green*

The history of the development of Spencers Wood is the story of a rural area which started as a common serving a sparse and impoverished farming community, which steadily grew as national prosperity increased and then developed into a bustling village. The countryside, with wooded hills and fields down to the River Loddon, is the backdrop to the main road which has been the focus of activity even when it was a mere track over the common. Through the centuries gossip and goods arrived along the road and the growing population absorbed new ideas, so that during late Georgian and Victorian times new trades and enterprises could flourish. Spencers Wood retained its identity as one of the separate villages in Shinfield parish. School, church and social life often turned north, west and south to other villages (Three Mile Cross, Grazeley, Swallowfield and Riseley) more readily than east to Shinfield village. This chapter describes how Spencers Wood has developed along the Basingstoke Road. It complements the information in Chapter One and in our earlier book, *Our Village of Spencers Wood*, published in 2001, and sets out the background for the remaining chapters of this book.

### Gradual Development up to 1800

The earliest known settlement in the Shinfield/Spencers Wood area was in Anglo-Saxon times. Domesday Book, compiled after the Norman conquest, in about 1087, records that Shinfield had previously been held by Sexi from King Edward the Confessor. It continues:

> There is land for six ploughs. [There are] eight villeins and five borders with seven ploughs. There are two serfs and a mill worth five shillings and 150 eels and five fisheries worth 550 eels and sixteen acres of meadow and woodland to render ninety swine. It was worth seven pounds now eight pounds.

This was an insignificant area on the western edge of Windsor Forest. The River

Loddon, which was its main asset, was navigable and provided food, water and power for mills to grind corn. Under Norman rule all land was held by the king who granted it to his favourites. Lands at Spencers Wood and Shinfield were frequently linked together as grants by successive kings who used the woodlands as hunting grounds. (It is interesting that there are still a few deer roaming in Spencers Wood.) In the first half of the thirteenth century Geoffrey le Despenser held half a knight's fee in the manor of Beaumys (partly in Shinfield and partly in Swallowfield) under the Earl of Warwick, and this may be the origin of the name 'Spencers Wood'. The church on the hill in Shinfield was the local centre, with any early village settlement nearby on the well-drained land.

Villagers grazed cattle on the damp fields and took timber and small wood products from the many woods and copses. Also they worked on the open-field farming system, where each man had scattered strips. They all had to co-operate in deciding the rotation of crops and sharing the oxen to draw the plough. Most men were bound to work the land of the lord of the manor, which was in the east of the parish, away from Spencers Wood. The Black Death of 1348 and other recurrent plagues during the fourteenth century left a shortage of farm labour, which provided the opportunity for those who remained to amalgamate their strips and manage the land for themselves. Gradually, increased prosperity enabled more farmers to become independent, and for tradesmen to make a living serving the small local community.

There is not much good farmland in Spencers Wood and many people were poor. The Poor Law was introduced to help, and here, established farmers like Mr Pither and Mr Body were Overseers of the Poor and paid much of the poor rate themselves. In the 1700s one scheme provided land or parish cottages on the edge of the common at Spencers Wood, where families could grow vegetables and keep pigs and geese, but life was hard there. Poor squatter families might still build houses of gorse and birch. Rural poverty became an acute national problem during the late eighteenth and early nineteenth centuries. In the 1770s a new workhouse for the poor was built at Great Lea common just north of Spencers Wood. People hated having to go there, and preferred to take 'outdoor relief', in which the Overseers provided items like 'a truss of straw to lie on', shoes, smocks, coals, and even coffins.

### The Lively Village of the nineteenth century

Mary Russell Mitford (1787–1855) wrote about local village life in articles that were published in the London magazine, *The Lady*. She lived in Three Mile Cross from 1820 to 1850 and described much of the countryside as she walked through the commons and along the lanes. Some of the trades such as bootmakers, carpenters and blacksmiths that she mentioned were established in Spencers Wood to supply local farmers. She described the travellers passing through Hampshire from the coast at Portsmouth, and going on down the Thames Valley at Reading. The main road was just a track across the open common when she was writing. It was one of many footpaths along which she walked.

Woodcock Lane is shown on early maps such as John Rocque's (1761) and Thomas Pride's (1790) to be as significant and useful as the lane that is now the Basingstoke Road. The former was a straight and level route south from Three Mile Cross on the west side of the hills forming Spencers Wood Common. The maps show that the rough land of the Common stretched on both sides of the Basingstoke road from the top of the hill south as far as Back Lane. No formal roads crossed it, and both Hyde End Road and Clares Green Road ended at its eastern edge. The present Recreation Ground was part of the Common. Small tracks and lanes went between Spencers Wood and Grazeley, and when Grazeley parish church was built in 1850, the new ecclesiastical parish of Grazeley included much of Spencers Wood. (Part of Spencers Wood was administered with Grazeley into the twentieth century.) Lacking a church, a non-conformist chapel was established in 1816 (see Chapter Five).

In the early nineteenth century, travel by land remained restricted especially in bad weather, and there are frequent references to local flooding in Mary Russell Mitford's writings. She relates how the two routes south from Three Mile Cross were surveyed for improvement by Mr McAdam in the 1830s and 1840s. He decided that the low road, Woodcock Lane, was less suitable than the route over the hill, and therefore created the paved route we have today. The new road had a much better surface than it had had previously, but it was generally rough with loose gravel and was frequently potholed, so it required frequent maintenance. Spencers Wood now had a better road into Reading and a chance for goods and people to move around with greater ease. (Woodcock Lane became a local footpath and byway; eventually land adjacent to it was chosen for the dual-carriageway by-pass from the M4 junction.)

About the middle of the nineteenth century, Spencers Wood gained its first public house, the Red Lion (see p. 41), which stood roughly opposite the Post Office close to the junction with Beech Hill Road. At first its trade may have been largely people travelling between Reading and the south, but when its licence was considered by the magistrates in 1867, they acknowledged the need for a hostelry had grown with the building of many small houses around Spencers Wood.

Two substantial gentry houses were built close to Spencers Wood. The early history of Highlands and the identity of its builder is far from clear but we know it had been erected by the early 1820s: it is still a landmark today

(Chapter Four). In 1859, Stanbury House, now demolished (see Chapter Six) was built for Frederick Allfrey; it stood on the brow of the hill with views over the Kennet valley to the west. Cottages were provided for his workers. Chapter One describes how he and other landowners were influential in the enclosure of Spencers Wood Common in 1863–65 – a very late enclosure date – although the arable fields had been enclosed earlier. Because the newly enclosed land on the western side of the road was largely acquired by the Highlands and Stanbury estates, the new building was mostly on the eastern side of the road (as shown on the 1899 edition of the Ordnance Survey map: see p. 9), and that remains the case through to this day. As the population grew, there was a need for a school in the area. Demand was first met by a school privately funded by Mrs Merry of Highlands – apparently from the mid-1850s – which had 40 pupils in 1890 when its teacher retired. In 1889–90 Mr Allfrey of Stanbury donated land and had a school built with a schoolteacher's house attached, and Mrs Merry's school moved there in the autumn of 1890. (This building later became the local library and the house became private property: see Chapter Nine.)

Spencers Wood had become a coherent village. Most men worked either on the land as labourers, or on the estates of the larger houses in the neighbourhood, and most women worked 'in service' for the landed families. There were also bakers, gardeners, wheelers and harness makers for the carts and carriages. Towards the end of the nineteenth century prosperous businessmen and professional people built their homes in Spencers Wood, away from the pollution and crowding of Reading. 'Modern' spacious properties were built in late Victorian and Edwardian times, usually of local Reading bricks and featuring the special cream or silver-finished bricks to mark out doorways, windows and other special elements. These buildings are a characteristic feature of the built landscape of Spencers Wood and are prominent along Basingstoke Road and in The Square. Other new houses, for example on Spencers Wood hill, used stonework and hanging tiles as their special feature.

House with patterned brickwork (1880s or '90s)

Towards the end of the nineteenth century the census returns and directories list more trades, catering for a population with some spare time, money, and aspirations. Service

Houses featuring expensive cream brickwork: 1880s or '90s (*left*); mid-1920s (*right*)

Sant's General Store (*left*), now Spencers Wood Stores (*right*)

providers for agriculture such as farriers (blacksmiths) and alehouses were gradually supplemented by shops selling food and other goods. A Post and Telegraph Office was established in one of the village houses near the junction with the road to Beech Hill, opposite the Red Lion ale house, which also sold 'fine wines and spirits'. Small manufacturing concerns were established nearby, such as Hewitt and Beken, carriage makers, and Sant's general store, draper's shop and café (later London House Stores and now Spencers Wood Stores). In The Square, Double's the blacksmiths now also repaired bicycles, and a harness and saddle-maker was established in the village. Carters provided transport, both by traditional horse and cart and also by new motor omnibuses: Cordery's ran a

local bus service with 'The Pride of the Valley' coaches. The kiln on the west side of the village supplied bricks for new houses, extensions and outbuildings, and local builders also used the bricks to line the wells. Judd's sawmill dealt with timber from the woods, advertising at the Post Office and at Sant's general store. When the Spencers Wood Institute opened in March 1894 offering a whole range of facilities and entertainments, the village could be said to have come of age (see Chapter Five).

### *Consolidation in the early twentieth century*

In 1903 a new building for the non-conformist congregation was constructed in a prominent position beside the main road at its junction with Hyde End Road. The growth in population in this part of the county was recognised by Berkshire County Council, which purchased land just past the southern boundary of the parish and built a school for the children of Spencers Wood and the surrounding area. It was opened in 1908 as the Swallowfield County School, but was soon renamed as the Spencers Wood Lambs Lane School. The Church of England was prompted by the presence of the Congregational Church to act on its own behalf, and build the Church of St Michael and All Angels on the brow of the hill; the first services were held there in 1908. St Michael's Hall was completed in 1911; this now belongs to the village and has always been well used (see Chapter Eleven).

The Village Hall and the church of St Michael and All Angels, at the top of Spencers Wood Hill

With the vastly improved roads and available public transport, as well as bicycles and a few early motor cars, people were able to move around much more, and maintain contact with nearby villages and the local towns of Reading and Wokingham. Regular coach and motor bus services to Reading took over from the horse and cart transport, although the latter continued to be used for local deliveries from shops and farms for many years. People living in Spencers Wood kept good social contact with friends and relatives in Grazeley and Three Mile Cross, and in the small nearby settlement of Ryeish Green. It was in the latter area that the new larger school was opened in 1910, initially as an all-age village school. Meanwhile more houses were built, especially along the main road, and the population slowly grew through the first half of the twentieth century.

## 1940s and 1950s

It was a mainly self-contained village that the evacuees found when they were brought here during the Second World War. In 1938 Shinfield civil parish had been designated as a 'reception area' for people evacuated from towns which were probable targets for enemy shelling and bombing. Teachers and pupils from several primary schools in the London area arrived in Spencers Wood in September 1939, and more followed in 1940, '41, and '42. Some moved on to other parts of the country and a few returned home, but some stayed; altogether, 65 children from 39 schools came to Spencers Wood. They were 'fitted in' at Lambs Lane School and were billeted at homes in the village. Our book about Lambs Lane School describes how most of these 'townies' loved the freedom of village life. During these years, especially as many men were away on war service, there was a large preponderance of children in the village, and many activities were introduced to occupy them after school hours.

The supply of what are now considered essential services had barely reached Spencers Wood before the outbreak of the war in 1939 stopped any further development. There was little mains electricity or street lighting, no mains water or gas supply. Water was drawn from wells or was pumped from underground, oil was delivered for lamps to provide lighting, gas for cooking was delivered as bottled, and coal and wood fuel for heating were delivered by local merchants.

After the end of the war in 1945, the acute shortage of housing meant that Nissen huts, which had been erected along the drive to Stanbury House for temporary occupation by prisoners of war, were improved and used for housing local people. They were mostly demolished in the 1950s, although some remained until 1964 (see p. 167). By that time Spencers Wood was a slowly growing community with several small shops including two butchers, and some general stores including a Co-operative Store, mostly scattered along the east side of the main road. Limited new development occurred, often on individual plots, for example, near the top of Hyde End Road. In the 1950s a tradition became established whereby people purchased a plot of land on which to build their own house, as wartime controls on the use of building materials were eased. Gradually gaps between houses were filled in, and some back gardens were built on. At this time however the dominant land use was still market gardening, especially behind the houses on the eastern side of Basingstoke Road, with some quite large orchards surrounding the housing, for example between Hyde End Road and Clares Green Road.

## Increasing Pace of Development after 1960

In the 1960s and 1970s services and infrastructure were upgraded and the pace of house building quickened, especially after the section of the M4 to the south of Reading, including junction 11, was opened in 1971. Spencers Wood had doubled in size in the 1960s, generally by infilling around existing properties. A series of new planning documents were produced by the government and by the Berkshire County Council, proposing ways in which development would be accommodated. In 1969 the *Spencers Wood Village Plan* was published by Berkshire County Council. This showed a tightly drawn village envelope to contain further building and a 'proposed new road' where the by-pass was to go. Shortly afterwards, the dual carriageway was built, to take through traffic away from the village. In the following years, two small office units were erected along Basingstoke Road, and housing was built, for example, along Beech Hill

Orchards were taken out in the 1970s for housing: Appletree Lane and Orchard Close were built on the site of the large orchard to the south of Clares Green Road, which you can see in the 1931 aerial photo on p. 83

Housing at Clements Close on the south side of the 'Common', built in the 1970s

Road at Clements Close and from Montgomery Drive along Larchfield towards Basingstoke Road. Businesses such as the sawmills, the brickworks and the motorworks had already closed, and as shopping habits changed in favour of supermarkets, some of the small shops shut down too.

## Residents' Association

In 1971, Spencers Wood formed part of the government's 'South East Area 8', and was earmarked for major growth. In the late 1960s, local residents had reacted to the calls for more development by forming the Spencers Wood and District Residents' Association. This was headed by Mr Harry Cook of Sussex Lane, Mr Ozzie Evans of Three Mile Cross, and Mr Barry Holden of Spencers Wood. The concerns and the aims of the Association have carried forward through the years as residents have tried to influence the changes and guidelines for extra building. The aims were to retain the separation between the settlements of Ryeish Green, Spencers Wood and Three Mile Cross, and as far as possible, to safeguard and enhance the features of the natural environment, while highlighting the existing inadequacies of the public utilities (water, electricity and so on) and the roads both within the parish and beyond, never mind their ability to cope with extra demands. Flooding from run-off over the clay ground of the hills as well as from rising levels of ground water from the Loddon has frequently been mentioned. Residents have always been concerned about the need for sufficient school places at primary and secondary level, and provision for very young children and after-school activities. The Association would make these points when responding to planning applications and at public inquiries on development proposals. The Association lapsed in the late 1970s but was revived in 1982 in response to further pressures.

## *County Council Structure Plans and Developers' Proposals*

By the beginning of the 1980s, however, the proximity of Spencers Wood to the M4 and to Reading, with its employment, its rail service to London and easy access to Heathrow, and the growth of high-tech businesses in the Thames Valley, had attracted the interest of the major house-building firms. In the late 1970s Berkshire County Council produced a Structure Plan for Central Berkshire proposing new areas for housing and associated development. This included land around Spencers Wood. In 1984, the Structure Plan for the whole county included Spencers Wood in an 'Area of Opportunity', a vast stretch of land that gave rise to talk of 'Readingstoke', with all the land from Reading to Basingstoke being covered with houses,

Small-scale industrial development (Wellington and Heron Industrial Estates)

The Red Lion Inn (*right*); now converted into two cottages with houses beside and behind it in Anvil Close (*below*)

Homes and community facilities provided for elderly people at Spring Gardens

roads, and infrastructure. It was proposed that there would be an additional 3000 houses, with an industrial/commercial complex between Church Lane in Three Mile Cross and the M4, with a major shopping centre and a fly-over across the motorway.

Since that time there have been many applications to build in Spencers Wood and all other parts of Shinfield parish, and local residents have countered with their own suggestions and (usually) objections to major development. Objections have frequently been taken to the limit through the planning system to public inquiries. Some inquiries resulted in applications being turned down, such as the plan to construct a major new development west of Spencers Wood in Grazeley. However, much land in Spencers Wood now became 'white land', where house builders have first option to buy while they attempt to get planning permission.

By the end of the twentieth century new housing had been built off Clares Green Road, along Hyde End Road and Basingstoke Road, with much infilling at the rear of housing. The main pattern of roads remained constant, however, with Basingstoke Road the only north-south through road, and Hyde End Road the only through east-west route. Housing developments were built on culs-de-sac off these two roads. The small ancient lanes of Croft Road, Ryeish Lane and Hyde End Lane remained small tarmac roads without footways but mostly with grass verges and ditches along both sides. To general delight, these are now a one-way traffic system.

### Major Development in the present day

Land on the east of Basingstoke Road and on fields between Hyde End Road and Ryeish Green is designated for many dwellings, and in the early twenty-first century these areas were selected as part of the 'South of the M4' Strategic Development Location, to provide at least 2500 new homes. By 2015, the

character of the area had become 'suburban', with more street lighting and security lighting to private properties, footways beside the roads with hard kerb edgings, but no undergrounding of the existing telephone and electricity wires on major roads. It is noticeable that in the recent developments, the smaller housing schemes have tended to be two-storey, detached homes with garages and gardens. In contrast, the larger developments have a higher density of dwellings. This includes varying proportions of apartments and terraced properties, often two-and-a-half or three storeys in height. Space for car parking is often very limited. However the housing areas have communal open grass spaces and specially designed and equipped play areas for children, and retain small copses and open water-courses where possible. The levy paid by builders is put towards

Open space left in Benham Drive (*above*); play equipment at the Recreation Ground (*below*)

Large-scale house building by the 'South of the M4 Consortium' began with the 'Croft Gardens' development in 2015

funding infrastructure and community requirements, such as improvements to existing services and schools.

Major new developments that started in 2015 are changing the scale and character of Spencers Wood from semi-rural to suburban, but it is hoped that the country setting and open views with footpaths into the countryside will continue to be appreciated by all its residents.

## Author's note

This chapter is based on the following sources: 'Parishes: Swallowfield', in *VCH Berkshire*, iii, pp. 267–74; Archive material from the Spencers Wood and District Residents' Association, in the possession of SWLHG; *Our Villages: Character Statement for Ryeish Green, Spencers Wood and Three Mile Cross* (2008); *Planning: What are your views?* (Berkshire County Council, 1984); *Structure Plan* (Berkshire County Council, 1988); *Shinfield Parish Community Plan* (2011); *Shinfield Parish Neighbourhood Plan* (forthcoming, 2017).

# CHAPTER FOUR

# Highlands

*Barry Boulton*

Highlands is a large gentleman's house which stands just on the edge of Spencers Wood, with a long approach from the Basingstoke Road. It is not easy to see from the main road and many will be unaware of its scale and grandeur. It is now used as the corporate headquarters of Nortons Chartered accountants (who in 2016 were acquired by and incorporated into Vistra International Expansion Limited), but the nineteenth-century inhabitants of the house played an important role in the development of Spencers Wood.

The earliest reference found so far to Highlands as a place-name comes from 1686 when the bounds of Bealmes manor noted Highlands Corner as a landmark on Woodcock Lane.[1] This is important, for it shows that Highlands is the name of an area rather than simply the name of a nineteenth-century house. In fact it is nearly a century before we can begin to thicken out the history of either the house or the larger space in which it sits.

The first cartographic evidence we have for the area around Highlands comes from Rocque's map of 1761. This shows a large close with Woodcock Lane to the west and Kiln Lane to the south. To the east the Highlands enclosure is separated from the common by a roughly triangular enclosure which has two buildings on it. This enclosure turns out to be important for the history of Highlands. No buildings are shown in the Highlands enclosure although there is a barn still standing at Highlands dated 1756. In 1771 the Bealmes court rolls recorded the conveyance of 'a barn and a parcel of land called Highlands' from the daughters of the late Mrs Philps (Mrs Rutledge and Mrs Parker) and their husbands, to one H. Palmer.[2] Thereafter we can trace the ownership (and occupation) of Highlands from 1780 through to 1832 using the Land Tax returns deposited with the Clerk of the Peace.[3] Key here is the Land Tax Redemption Certificate made in 1799. This identifies a cottage, farm and barn in the township of Shinfield in Wiltshire called Highlands belonging to George Jennings and paying Land Tax of £1 12s. 0d.[4] Knowing the owner at the end of the eighteenth century and the amount he paid, it is then easy to trace the property back to 1780 and forwards to 1832 in the annual Land Tax returns.

These show that Robert Palmer Esq. was the owner in 1780 and continued so until 1797: Jennings paid the Land Tax from 1798. Palmer had the property in the hands of tenants, first one John Wight and then one Thomas Pither but Jennings always had the land in hand. Highlands was offered for sale in June 1797 as:

> a barn and stable adjoining with five closes of arable land containing 41a 3r 27p or thereabouts called Highlands situated in the parish of Shinfield in the occupation of farmer Thomas Pither.[5]

George Jennings may be the grocer and bacon seller of Broad Street in Reading who retired from business in June 1795 and directed his goodwill to one Joshua Vine. He may also be the man of that name, described as simply George Jennings of Reading gent. who made his will in 1818, proved in 1825, but by this time there is nothing in the will to connect this Jennings with the Jennings of Highlands.[6] But he was for a time the tenant of the Hunter family's farm at Spencers Wood and for that reason a much more substantial figure than appears from the Land Tax.[7]

We then need to consider the advertisement placed in a London paper in March 1818:

> Five enclosures of highly-improveable arable and pasture land, ornamented with young thriving timber, consisting of 20a 3r 28p very pleasantly situate in the village of Shinfield, four miles from Reading and about 39 miles from London, contiguous to the estate purchased for the Duke of Wellington: a most delightful spot to build either a cottage or mansion, commanding uninterrupted views over Oxfordshire and Hampshire hills, in a good sporting part of the country, where several packs of hounds are kept.[8]

The timing, the description of the location, and the fact that the property was in Shinfield in Wiltshire makes it almost certain that it was Highlands that was being offered, but not all of it: note that in 1797 the acreage was just short of 42 acres and the 1818 sale notice includes no buildings. And yet there is room for doubt. The sale notices of 1797 and 1818 all refer to five closes. Highlands is close to, but hardly 'contiguous' with, the Duke's estate. There is either a typographical error in the advertised acreage, or the intention was to divide the property. The Land Tax points to the whole of Jennings' property being sold as one unit: there is no sign that it was divided. This all seems to be inconsistent but an explanation is possible.

At this moment we should review the map evidence. Pride's map is quite clear that there was no building on the site of the modern Highlands *c*.1790. Nor is there any house at Highlands on the preliminary sketches for the first edition Ordnance Survey made in 1792.[9] It is likely that Jennings built a smaller house, the cottage mentioned in the redemption certificate, and it is not impossible that this stood on the part of Highlands not offered for sale in 1818, but at the moment it is impossible to say one way or another.

The purchaser from Jennings was one John Carter. We know that Carter died on 1 May 1820 and was buried at Beenham, thus tying him to the Carter family of Beenham House. The *Reading Mercury* noted that he was of Highlands but died at his house in Southampton Street, aged 54.[10] His death may have been sudden: there appears to be no will. Why Carter built a house here, and what his source of income was is something of a mystery. Whether he is the man of that name who joined with Richard Body in securing an enclosure of the common on which to build a Sunday School in 1815 is not clear: in the account of the foundation of the school (out of which the Congregational Church developed), he is called John Carter Esq. of Shinfield (see p. 56). The same account makes it clear that he had died by 1825.[11]

Although there is no explicit statement, it does seem most likely that Carter was the builder of the house we know today as Highlands. We know for certain that the mansion existed soon after his death. Whether he lived to enjoy it is doubtful, and we have to suppose that his widow was confronted with a house that was too big for her purposes, but which also perhaps represented the dashed hopes of a life there with her late husband. There is a further argument for Carter being the probable builder of the house: the rentals of the Hunter estate show that by 1817 a John Carter held Clappers Farm in Beech Hill at a quit rent of 5*s*., but he was also paying £5 rent for 'land taken from the waste at front of his house at Spencers Wood waste, old brick kiln Spencers Wood'. This appears in several different formulations over the years: in the 1823 rental it is described as 'a brick kiln formerly standing near Highlands'. Elsewhere the same property is described as:

> a piece or parcel of ground situate and lying and being in Spencers Wood ... on part of which a brick kiln formerly stood and which parcel or piece of land is now laid into the garden and premises belonging to the house late of Carter.

The site of the old brick kiln was sold to Mrs Carter in the mid-1820s and disappears from the rentals.[12]

It seems probable that the brick kiln and the land on which it stood was the triangular enclosure shown on Rocque's map, which is still visible on the

Tithe Map, 1838 (BRO D/D1 110/1B)

tithe map as closes 583 (to the east of the house), 584 (the lodge now demolished), 585 and 586. It is obvious enough why Carter wanted to acquire this land – it stood between the common and his new house and a brick kiln was surely not what he wanted to pass on his way home!

How do we make sense of this? We can speculate that Carter acquired the southern part of the Highlands enclosure at some point in the 1810s and began to build a house. The northern part was later offered for sale as a house site with land: Carter also acquired that too if only to protect his privacy and ambience. He probably bought the lease of the brick kiln which stood close to his house, in order to close it down and demolish it, and its lands were finally purchased and incorporated into the grounds of Highlands.

As we saw, Carter did not live to enjoy his house for long and his widow returned to Southampton Street where she died in 1827. The house was let to Captain (later Admiral) John Mackellar from around 1821. Mackellar's colourful career started in Minorca in 1766, where his father, Col. Patrick Mackellar, was building the defences of the island. Both he and his brother, Neil, later Colonel, were born on the island, 'begat on the body of Mrs Elizabeth Lezain wid'. John Mackellar joined the navy in 1781, after his education in Scotland; he served on many ships including HMS *Victory* before getting his own command of HMS *Terpsichore* in 1801, but in 1802 he was dismissed from the service for 'scandalous, cruel and oppressive conduct.' He was reinstated in 1804 after he received praise in high places for his previous service. He was then appointed Agent for Prisoners of War and Governor of the Naval Hospital at Halifax, Nova Scotia, where he remained for six years. On his return to England he found no ship to command and spent two years trying to join the Spanish Navy. In 1813 Captain Mackellar sold 'Orchard Cottage', his house at Tor (Tormoham) in Devon, and left with 19-year-old Mary Eales, a girl from the village, for St Pancras in London, where she bore him the first two of ten children. The Captain then moved to Highlands before their third child was born in 1821 (the child being baptised at Shinfield church). Three more children were also born while the family was living here, including Flora Irene Campbell, their fifth child, who died aged six months and was buried at Shinfield. As a widower – his wife having died two months earlier in Tor – he

'Highlands', South and south east aspect, 1911 (BRO D/EX 2238/1/26) The carriage drive, about one third of a mile in length, 1911 (BRO D/EX 2238/1/26)

finally married Mary Eales in London in 1828. His last four children were born in Boulogne. The Mackellars were still occupying Highlands in August 1827 when an advertisement says that vacant possession could be obtained, but it seems likely that they left in October of that year. The *Berkshire Chronicle* has a notice of a sale of the contents of the house to be held on 10 October 1827 including its works of art, furniture, library and farm gear and farm stocks.[13] Mackellar's connection with Highlands ended in 1827, but he continued his advancement through the ranks, being made Vice-Admiral in 1837 and full Admiral in 1847 by which time he was nearing eighty. He died at Cheltenham aged 86 in 1854.[14]

When the Highlands Estate was put up for sale in 1827 it was described as:

> A very superior modern built residence of handsome elevation, with lawn, well planted pleasure ground, productive garden and fourty-two acres of arable and pasture land. The house contains seven airy bedrooms, dining and drawing rooms, breakfast parlour, entrance with portico, butler's pantry, housekeepers room, domestic offices and cellars. Detached offices in a large yard comprise a four-stall stable, coach house, barn and Dutch granary, other outbuildings and a valuable right of common. To be sold or let on a term of 3, 5, 7 years.[15]

Whether the house failed to sell in 1827, or a purchaser got cold feet and wanted to sell the property on is unknown, but it was advertised again in April 1828 as being either for sale or available to lease for three, five or seven years.[16] And whether William Merry bought it at this moment, or shortly after, cannot be discovered. He first appears in the Land Tax in 1831, but he was well-established in Shinfield and other local affairs by 1833.[17]

William Merry (1792–1873) was the elder son of William Merry (d. 1855), Undersecretary of State for the War Department from 1810 to 1825. William Merry junior served as Private Secretary to Palmerston from 1812 to 1828. He was educated at Winchester, and married Anne, the second daughter of Kender Mason of Beel-House in Buckinghamshire in 1820. On his retirement from Palmerston's service, he bought Highlands and was certainly resident there by 1831. The Merry connection with Highlands then lasted to 1911 when his adopted daughter died and the house and estate was sold.[18]

William Merry, as a man of independent means, devoted his life to public service and local administration. As was said at the time of his death, 'He may ... be said to have devoted himself almost entirely to the discharge of duties which he had undertaken for the benefit of the public'.[19] First and foremost of these was that he was a prominent and active magistrate and served as one of the visiting magistrates for Reading gaol. When nominated to be Sheriff of Berkshire in 1867, he petitioned the Privy Council to be released from his nomination, as being sheriff was incompatible with his other duties, and this was finally agreed.[20] Locally he was prominent in societies devoted to improving the lives of working men although not all of these seem to have been long-lived. He appears to have been the prime mover in the Shinfield Agricultural and Labourers Friend Society, and the Shinfield Agricultural Association. The latter, holding its annual show and ploughing competition at the end of May 1846 at Three Mile Cross, moved to Hill House (with the accompaniment of a brass band) for dinner and prize-giving in one of the barns. As the *Reading Mercury* reported:

> The rewards were afterwards distributed by William Merry Esq., the chairman, who, at the conclusion, expressed a hope that he should see them all at church in their new clothes on Sunday 7th of June, when he should be happy to present each of them with a Testament. Mrs Merry, Miss Mitford, and the other ladies took the liveliest interest in the proceedings and the former lady [Mrs Merry] was exceedingly attentive to the wants of the labourers whilst at dinner. ... the success which attended [the day] was the result of the noble and praiseworthy exertions of the highly respected chairman Mr Merry.[21]

Miss Mitford is of course Mary Russell Mitford, with whom Merry is known to have been on friendly terms, exchanging plants with her. Merry was also active in evangelical circles, being an active supporter of the Church Missionary Society and the Church Pastoral Aid Society[22] and published three books discussing aspects of Christianity, which inspired Elizabeth Barrett Browning.[23]

Merry's interests in the improvement of society and his evangelical Christianity came together in the building of Holy Trinity Church, Grazeley, erected in 1850. Merry subscribed to the costs of the building, served as secretary of the committee that oversaw its erection and when the Bishop of Oxford laid the foundation stone in 1849, he travelled over from Highlands and returned to have dinner there.[24] Merry is said to have presented the church with an organ that he occasionally played himself. He acted as a patron for Grazeley School: in 1870 and doubtless other years, the children came over to Highlands for a day of entertainments, races and meals.[25] Merry left money in his will to provide a salary for the schoolmistress or master of Grazeley School of £23, £7 p.a. towards the maintenance of Grazeley School and the teacher's house, £20 p.a. to be given in clothing to the schoolchildren of Grazeley at Christmas and £40 p.a. to the poor of Grazeley.[26]

Hence it comes as no surprise that Highlands and all the land to the west of the Basingstoke Road formed part of the new parish of Grazeley and were not transferred to the new parish of Spencers Wood in 1913. But Merry also sponsored good works in Spencers Wood itself. He and his wife maintained a school, apparently in the inner lodge (now demolished) on the common's edge. The students from the Merry's school joined those from Grazeley for the day of entertainments in 1870, and the school, then said to have been in existence for 35 years, continued through to the building of F. W. Allfrey's school in 1890, when the baton was passed from one Spencers Wood landowner to another.[27]

Moreover, Merry has had a lasting influence on the village. With the enclosure of Spencers Wood common in 1862, he purchased six plots of land from the lord of the manor, Henry Lannoy Hunter, John May and John Thorpe, so that he could retain access to the Basingstoke Road via a carriage drive. The Highlands estate therefore came to include all the land between Woodcock Lane in the west and the Basingstoke Road in the east, and this remains open ground, and will do so until the present owners release it for building. The gated entrance to the estate, situated opposite the junction with Hyde End Road (as you can see in the aerial view on p. 83),

The inner lodge and drive, near the residence, 1911. After Merry acquired part of the former common, this lodge was no longer needed and was used as a school (BRO D/EX 2238/1/26)

had a lodge that was occupied by one of the gardeners. This lodge has also been demolished, with houses built on the site, and the entrance was moved to its present position further along the Basingstoke Road.

Even though his wife was still living, Mr Merry left his house and property to his adopted daughter Henrietta Crowdy as he wished his wife to live free of worry, and trusted that Miss Crowdy would remain a loyal companion for her. Miss Crowdy seems to have done so, remaining at Highlands after the death of Mrs Merry in 1891, until she herself died in August 1911.[28] As a governor of Spencers Wood Infants' School, Miss Crowdy visited it to inspect the children's needlework and play the piano for them. At Christmas time all the children received gifts. Mr and Mrs Merry and Henrietta Crowdy are all buried in Grazeley Churchyard.

The contents of the house were auctioned in November 1911 and Highlands itself was auctioned on 12 December.[29] It was sold to a Yorkshire minerals owner, John Rowley Horton, who died whilst living at the house in 1924.[30] He made some alterations to it. The conservatory was removed and new bay windows were added to match the other bay windows. At some time before the mid-1930s the house was extended on the north side, with a new entrance.[31] The infants' school that had been at the inner gate was pulled down and a bungalow erected.[32] Mr Horton also installed a wind pump to bring water from the 'Hogswell' to a huge cistern in the roof of the house.

The next residents were Mrs Cookson and her daughter, followed by Major Maynard. Highlands was offered for sale by the Cooksons in 1933 and sold privately the following year.[33]

The purchaser was Maurice Fitzgerald Sandes Magill. Magill was from a family resident at Churchtown House, County Kerry, Ireland, He was educated at Fettes College, Edinburgh. In 1910 he went to India and later served with the Bombay Scottish Regiment. He married Constance Eveline Bibby in 1919. She was the younger daughter of A. W. Bibby of Liverpool, the Chairman of Bibby Line Ltd (est. 1840). Well-known in the neighbourhood for his kindness and generosity, Maurice Magill took a great deal of interest in local affairs. He was President of the Shinfield, Swallowfield and District Horticultural Society, whose annual show was held at Highlands in alternate years; Vice President of the local British Legion; Chairman of St Michael's Hall

M. F. S. Magill, Highlands, Spencers Wood (BRO Q/Z1/47)

Management Committee; Chairman of Spencers Wood Cricket Club; Governor of Grazeley School and Churchwarden at Grazeley Church. He was appointed High Sheriff of Berkshire in 1950. Mrs Magill served the community as a Justice of the Peace and organised many fund-raising events in the village. She was a Governor of Ryeish Green School: one of the school houses was named after her. As Chief Evacuation Officer for Spencers Wood during the Second World War, she found homes for the many evacuees who came to the village. Brian Terry, one of the evacuees, sometimes called in at Highlands and was always given a warm welcome and afternoon tea.[34] During the war Italian prisoners were brought in to help with the farm work. The local Fire Service was also based at Highlands with the Spencers Wood Platoon of the Home Guard, of which Mr Magill was Commanding Officer (see Chapter Thirteen).

After Mr Magill died on 1 March 1967,[35] the house and a few acres of land surrounding it were sold and the house was converted into offices. In the 1980s, a road in Spencers Wood was named Magill Close in honour of the family.

# Notes

[1] BRO D/EBB M 3 (unpaginated), perambulation of 1686.

[2] BRO D/EHR M 43, Bealmes court roll 9 Dec. 1771.

[3] The main series of Land Tax returns is at Wiltshire and Swindon Record Office, A1/345/365. There are a number of locally held copies for 1797–98 and 1800 in BRO, EBB/O3/6. The master set marked with the redemption numbers is in The National Archives (TNA), IR23/94, fo. 192r–v.

[4] TNA, IR 24/42, no. 30443.

[5] *Reading Mercury,* 26 June 1797.

[6] *Reading Mercury,* 29 June 1795; TNA, PROB 11/1703, fos. 313v–15r.

[7] See the lease of Body's Farm to Jennings at BRO, D/EFa T29.

[8] *Public Ledger and Daily Advertiser,* 19 Mar. 1818.

[9] BRO, T/M 28.

[10] *Reading Mercury,* 6 May 1820. He was buried in Beenham on 9 May (BRO, Beenham parish register transcript).

[11] BRO, D/N 44/6/2/1/1.

[12] BRO, EBB M2 *passim*; D/EHR T62 (an abstract of T41).

[13] *Berkshire Chronicle*, 6 Oct. 1827.

[14] *Cheltenham Chronicle*, 20 Apr. 1854.

[15] *Berkshire Chronicle*, 4 Aug. 1827.

[16] *Berkshire Chronicle*, 12 Apr. 1828.

[17] He was churchwarden of Shinfield in 1833, *Berkshire Chronicle*, 27 July 1833.

[18] BRO D/EX 2238/1/26, Illustrated sale catalogue of Highlands (90 a.), Spencers Wood.

[19] For obituaries, see *Reading Mercury* and *Berkshire Chronicle* 1 Feb. 1873; and the encomium at the Berkshire Easter sessions reported in *The Times*, 9 Apr. 1873.

[20] *Reading Mercury* 18 Nov. 1865, 19 Oct. 1867, 4 Jan. 1868.

[21] *Reading Mercury* 30 May 1846.

[22] For instance *Berkshire Chronicle* 4 Oct. 1856, *Reading Mercury* 1 Nov. 1856; 1 May 1858. Merry left £200 each to the Church Pastoral Aid Society and the Church Missionary Society, *Berkshire Chronicle,* 22 Mar. 1873.

[23] For notes on Merry, Browning and Mitford, see www.browningscorrespondence.com/biographical-sketches/?id=918

[24] *Berkshire Chronicle,* 21 Oct. 1843; 26 Apr. 1845; 8 Sept. 1849.

[25] *Berkshire Chronicle,*10 Sept. 1870.

[26] *Berkshire Chronicle,* 22 Mar. 1873.

[27] *Berkshire Chronicle,* 10 Sept. 1870; 16 Aug. 1890.

[28] *Reading Mercury,* 26 Aug. 1911.

[29] *Reading Mercury,* 4 Nov., 9 Dec. 1911;

[30] For Horton see the death notice in *The Times*, 3 Oct. 1924. In the 1911 census he was living at Sharrow Grange in Sheffield.

[31] Museum of English Rural Life, University of Reading, Black and white photographic negatives of Spencers Wood, Berkshire sub-series P DX323 PH1/E169, "Highlands", Spencer's Wood (C926). These photographs were taken by Philip Osborne Collier, 1881–1979, photographer, between 1905 and the mid-1930s.

[32] BRO, D/EX 2238/1/26, "Highlands", Spencers Wood (Nicholas, 1911).

[33] *The Times*, 8 Sept, 24 Oct. 27 Nov. 1933, 1 Mar. 1934.

[34] Brian Terry, *The Days Were Always Sunny* (unpublished manuscript, copy in possession of Spencers Wood Local History Group).

[35] *The Times*, 2 Mar. 1967.

## CHAPTER FIVE

# The Congregational Church

*Mary K. Wheway*

This chapter is based on the references cited as well as the memories of many people who attended the Church.

## The First Chapel

Before 1815, there was no place of worship in the village of Spencers Wood and two gentlemen of the village decided that this situation should be remedied. John Carter gained permission from Henry Lannoy Hunter and the freeholders to enclose 40 poles (¼ acre) of land near the milestone on Spencers Wood Common, to erect a building for a Sunday School and divine worship at the joint expense of himself and Richard Body. William Bromley, a baker and grocer in Three Mile Cross wrote in 1824 that John Norris fenced the land, Thomas Jones was responsible for the carpentry and George Stone the brickwork for the building, which had been finished in April 1816 and first used on 5 May 1816.[1]

In order for Protestant dissenters to use the building for religious purposes, it had to be registered with the local bishop. This was duly done in 1817:

> Whereas it has been duly certified to the Lord Bishop of Sarum that a certain building erected and situated at Spencers Wood in the parish of Shinfield in the county of Berkshire and diocese of Sarum is intended forthwith to be used as a Sunday School and place of religious worship by an assembly or congregation of Protestants. I do therefore hereby certify that the certificate there of hath been duly registered and recorded in the registry of the said Bishop pursuant to the directions of an Act of Parliament made and passed in the fifty second year of his present Majesty's reign as witness my hand this twenty ninth day of May in the year of our Lord one thousand eight hundred and seventeen.
>
> C. I. W. Davies<br>Diocesan Registrar[2]

W. H. Summers mentions the chapel in his book on the history of Congregational churches in the area (1905), and says that Mr James Rodway had charge of this chapel, as well as the Baptist chapel at Beech Hill. 'He was there in 1818, and also in 1835', Summers says. Summers goes on to say that the 'chapel on the present site perhaps took the place of this older sanctuary, and *appears to date from 1837*'. However, in an *affidavit* signed in 1865, the above-mentioned William Bromley, then aged 71, recalled that 'in and about the year 1816 the present building which *has ever since been used as a chapel and school* of the Protestant Dissenters known as "Independents" was erected by the late Mr Richard Body ... and John Carter'. Perhaps the confusion stems from the will of Richard Body, made on 18 May 1837, in which he left £500 in support of the Sunday School, and left the school and premises to his wife, Ann Body. Richard Body died in 1842, and in her will of 1853 his widow left land for a Sunday School and a garden but she did not die until 1857. Although the Congregationalists certainly dated the start of their chapel as 1837, celebrating its centenary in 1937, there is no evidence that a new chapel was built then, but in 1885, a vestry, classroom and stable were built at a cost of £150.[3]

The old chapel (Mrs Wellstead with lawn-mower)

There are very few records about the life of the old chapel. We have a photograph of the exterior but the description of the interior relies on memories. Jack Povey wrote in 1937 that:

> it was a building with seating accommodation for about 200 people. The 'pews' were large hard forms and the 'Pulpitt' was a rostrum with a small platform. At the back of the Chapel was a high gallery with steps leading up to it.

He added, probably with a twinkle in his eye, that 'You can guess that some "exciting tales" could be told of those galleries by some of the old boys and girls'.[4] Mrs Ethel Lowe, the local Postmistress, wrote:

> In the old days, there were high backed pews, as in other places of worship. I think the lower seats of today are much nicer and a great improvement. I think the little people would be unable to see the preacher and perhaps it is as well the preacher could not see them.[5]

The first chapel held many special memories for its worshippers. There was reluctance on the part of some of the congregation to take the new church of

1903 to their hearts immediately: one couple, Mr Richards and Miss Ballard, decided to marry in the old chapel even though the new one was ready.

The old chapel was not demolished until the 1930s, when a resolution was passed at the Church Meeting of 21 June 1934:

> that the members were desirous, with the consent of the trustees, of erecting a manse on the whole or part of the site of the old church, utilising such material of the old building as may be serviceable and we agree that necessary steps be taken to this end.[6]

It was also proposed that in the event of a manse being built on the old site, a memorial stone be placed in the building to commemorate the date of the original building. Later the architect suggested a brass plate inside the manse rather than a stone memorial outside.[7]

## *The Institute*

In March 1894 the *Reading Mercury* reported that a 'Village Hall, or Iron Room' had been erected, 'just opposite the Chapel … for the purpose of an Institute and for meetings and entertainments'. The reference to an 'Iron Room' was because it was a prefabricated building made of corrugated iron, on a foundation laid by Edwin Wheeler; it was later referred to as the 'tin institute'. Mr Vernon Knowles and others connected with Trinity Congregational Church, Reading, were responsible for this: the total cost was £150, of which £100 had already been raised, £20 from Mr Body (presumably Richard Bernard Body). Mr W. Ravenscroft, architect, of Reading oversaw the erection of the building and 'also designed the tasteful internal decorations'. Before the opening ceremony there was a tea for 'all the men of the village'. Mr Morley of Padworth House presided over the meeting, congratulating them on having:

> such a useful hall, which he felt would be of lasting benefit to the neighbourhood, and would make life in their village brighter and happier. They would be able to meet there for social and friendly intercourse, and he hoped they would also use it for the purposes of discussing the great questions of the day, as well as for concerts and social gatherings.

Referring to the Parish Councils Bill, Mr Morley hoped that other villages would acquire 'rooms of a similar nature'. Mr Knowles announced that 'the room would be open each evening, when papers and games, etc, would be provided: and a "Pleasant Sunday Afternoon" would also be held there each week. A cricket club … was also to be established'. The following Wednesday, the Sunday School children gave an entertainment in 'the New Village Hall at Spencers Wood'.[8]

Unfortunately, this building only lasted five years: early one Friday morning in March 1899 it was found to be ablaze and had probably been burning all night, but no one knew the cause (Jack Povey wrote that 'it is thought that the heat of the sun was the cause of its setting on fire', but this seems unlikely). The Country Fire Office brigade were called out but 'the building was well alight … An ample supply of water was obtained from a pond near', which helped to prevent nearby cottages from igniting. The 'chairs, tables, books, piano, billiard and bagatelle tables, etc. were totally destroyed'. The Institute had been used by the young men of the church for their Bible classes, and classes under the 'umbrella' of the Adult School Movement, a movement which started in the 1790s but reached its peak in the run-up to the First World War. The young men were devastated at the loss of their building and at first they met in the kitchen of the local laundry but the landlord objected. Mrs Lowe the Postmistress (mother-in-law of Mrs Ethel Lowe) let them use her best room until the Institute was rebuilt.[9]

SPENCER'S WOOD INSTITUTE.

The Institute, architect's drawing

When the Institute burnt down, the church had just purchased some land for the building of a new church, and some land at the back was set aside for a new Institute. The young men of the village decided to rebuild the Institute themselves and they set about persuading friends to donate them the materials. Mr T. Talfourd Cummings, who was an articled pupil of a local architect, volunteered to act as Honorary Architect and drew out the plans and specifications. The young men of Spencers Wood, together with helpers from the congregation and from Trinity Congregational Church, Reading, completed the building within nine months. A report in the *Berkshire Chronicle* described it as:

> a handsome and commodious building … with a picturesque porch … of brick with stone finishings to the windows, which are glazed with lead lights in small squares. There is a large club room 44 feet long by 17 feet wide, with a small platform at one end. … The room has an open timber roof, and is lighted by four hanging lamps … It has a dado

around, above which neat brickwork is shown. This room will be used for games or as a reading room, and it is hoped if possible to arrange for gymnastics in it at an early date. There is a smaller room attached … 12 feet by 12 feet, and it has in it a small portable range, which will be used if necessary for refreshment purposes.[10]

The *Reading Observer,* too, reported on the opening ceremony. The Mayor of Reading (Mr A. H. Bull) performed the opening ceremony although the weather was 'unpropitious'. There was a large crowd, which was swelled by members of Trinity Church of Reading. At 3 o'clock there was a special service led by the Rev. Arthur Furner from Bristol and, at 5 o'clock, tea was served in a large marquee to about 150 people. Then at 7 o'clock, there was a public meeting to declare the Institute open. The young men did not forget the kindness of Mrs Lowe and presented her with a new carpet for her best room after their boots had trampled over her original carpet for over a year.[11] Shortly after the opening of the Institute, a village carnival and sale of work was held in aid of the furnishing fund for the Church and Institute.

The Institute in 1993

Spencers Wood had 'obtained a name for itself as a place where religious effort is whole-hearted and consequently successful'. Mrs C. F. Millett of The Crofts, 'a broad-minded Churchwoman, whose services to the village in various ways are spoken of very highly', both helped to organise and opened the event, which was described thus:

The visitor, turning just off the main road into the grounds of the Church and Institute, noticed the entrance gaily decorated with national flags; and then, entering the room, was surrounded with stalls heavily laden with the products of the loom and the needle; the fruits of the earth; the examples of the art of cuisinerie, at a vantage point where visitors 'sometimes counsel take – sometimes tea'; and a 'fish pond!' The stock of tastefully arranged articles of commerce were to be disposed of, and the manner of their disposal was that with which all have become familiar. Overhead the prettiness of the stalls was supplemented and

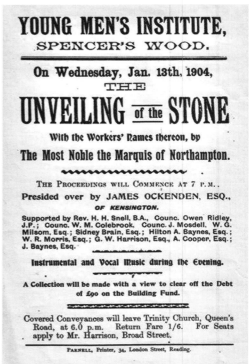

YOUNG MEN'S INSTITUTE,
SPENCER'S WOOD.

On Wednesday, Jan. 13th, 1904,

THE

UNVEILING of the STONE

With the Workers' Names thereon, by

The Most Noble the Marquis of Northampton.

THE PROCEEDINGS WILL COMMENCE AT 7 P.M.,

Presided over by JAMES OCKENDEN, ESQ.,
OF KENSINGTON.

Supported by Rev. H. H. Snell, B.A., Counc. Owen Ridley, J.P.; Counc. W. M. Colebrook, Counc. J. Mosdell, W. G. Milsom, Esq.; Sidney Brain, Esq.; Hilton A. Baynes, Esq.; W. R. Morris, Esq.; G. W. Harrison, Esq., A. Cooper, Esq.; J. Baynes, Esq.

Instrumental and Vocal Music during the Evening.

A Collection will be made with a view to clear off the Debt of £90 on the Building Fund.

Covered Conveyances will leave Trinity Church, Queen's Road, at 6.0 p.m.   Return Fare 1/6.   For Seats apply to Mr. Harrison, Broad Street.

PARNELL, Printer, 34, London Street, Reading.

Commemorative tablet of the young men who built the institute (from W. H. Summers, *History of the Berkshire, South Oxon, and South Bucks Congregational Churches* (1905), opp. p. 198.
Notice of the unveiling ceremony (*right*)

accentuated with coloured festoons of paper and at intervals Chinese lanterns. ... Master Sidney Double, a blue-eyed, fair-haired little fellow, prettily presented Mrs Millett with a bouquet.[12]

A couple of years later, in 1904, a commemorative stone tablet naming the young men who had worked so hard to build the Institute was unveiled by the Marquis of Northampton. Details of the ceremony are shown in the notice above. The tablet is now in the possession of the Spencers Wood Local History Group.

### *The Church of 1903*

Within three months of the opening of the new Institute in May 1902, more building was to start. The need for a new, larger church had long been felt and everything was now in place to start the building. At this time, Spencers Wood Congregational Church had affiliations with Trinity Congregational Church, Reading, which oversaw the ministry here. They were always on hand to support the activities here and Spencers Wood became a daughter church of Trinity. This meant they did not have a completely free hand with things like the new building and the choice of minister in charge.

Wednesday 9 July 1902 was an important day in the history of both churches: it was the day of two stone-laying ceremonies. Trinity Church was finally able to afford to build a wall around their church in Reading, to replace a wooden fence. This ceremony was at 3 o'clock and when it was over many people travelled to Spencers Wood to the stone-laying ceremony of the new church there. Mr Owen Ridley performed the stone laying, and Mr W. Ravenscroft handed him a parchment that was to be placed in a bottle under the foundation stone, recording 'the circumstances connected with the stone'. Mr Ridley read the message on the parchment to the assembled people:

> To the glory of God and for the extension of the kingdom of Christ on earth, this memorial stone of the Congregational Church, Spencers Wood, near Reading, is laid. ... Builder of the Church, Mr Edwin Wheeler.[13]

Mr Ridley was then handed a solid silver trowel with a pearl handle by the architect to perform the ceremony. The trowel was inscribed:

> Presented to Mr Owen Ridley, Esq., J.P., on the occasion of his placing the stone commemorating the erection of the new Congregational Church, Spencers Wood near Reading by the architects, Messrs Ravenscroft, Son and Morris, July 9th 1902.[14]

Immediately after the stone-laying ceremony, the anniversary meeting of Spencers Wood Sunday School was held. They were proud to announce that 'they had entered 29 new scholars to the Sunday School this year, bringing the total to 164'.[15]

The erection of this church was undertaken to supply a long-felt need, and to take the place of the smaller building hard by, in which the church and congregation at Spencers Wood had worshipped since at least 1837 if not 1817. The new building was erected by voluntary subscriptions in connection with the Congregational Twentieth Century Fund:

> The materials used are chiefly brick, tiles and wood, and the building consists of a nave and narrow aisles, chancel, vestry, tower, porch, storeroom and heating chamber. The interior is finished in red brick with cement dado and the roof is supported on large oak posts on hard stone bases, the roof being open timbered. The whole of the windows are in wood with leaded glass and the principal light is obtained by the ends and by dormer windows, which also serve for good ventilation. The tower forms a picturesque feature and provision is made in it for access to a small gallery to be erected at the end of the church when further accommodation is required.

Absence of 'style' has been sought rather than anything being definitely marked, the effort being to produce something very quiet, suitable to its purpose and in harmony with the country. This is provided by large sloping buttresses externally and a broad span of roof running over nave and aisles. The seating consists of open benches and accommodation is provided for 280 adults exclusive of future gallery, which will seat 50 persons. The dimensions of the church are 63 feet in length and 31 feet in breadth, and the work has been carried out by Mr Edwin Wheeler of Spencers Wood from the designs and under the supervision of Messrs Ravenscroft, Son and Morris, of Reading, the architects. The contract for the building amounted to £1,451. The land was purchased at the cost of £160. The cost of the church and the necessary laying out of the grounds will be about £1,700. Towards that amount, including the gifts on the stone, some £1,173 has been given or promised.[16]

Poster for the opening of the new Congregational church (1903)

## The New Congregational Church, SPENCERS WOOD.

### OPENING DAY, WEDNESDAY, JULY 15, 1903.

*The Opening Ceremonies will take place on the above date.*

**DIVINE SERVICE** will be held in the Afternoon at 3.30.
A Sermon will be preached by the REV. AMBROSE SHEPHERD, of Glasgow.

**TEA** will be served in the Institute at 5.15.

**A PUBLIC MEETING** will be held in the Evening at 7, presided over by HIS WORSHIP THE MAYOR OF READING. The REV. AMBROSE SHEPHERD will speak.

The following gentlemen are expected to be present: OWEN RIDLEY, Esq., J.P., WM. MCILROY, Esq., SYDNEY BRAIN, Esq., W. POULTON, Esq., J.P., the REVS. R. HERBERT SEWELL, B.A., WM. ARMSTRONG, M.A., SYDNEY TUCKER, of Henley-on-Thames, H. HERBERT SNELL, B.A., some of whom are expected to take part in the meeting.

*COLLECTIONS WILL BE TAKEN FOR THE BUILDING FUND.*

Brakes will run from Trinity at 2.30 and 6, returning from Spencers Wood at convenience. Return Fare 1/6 Tickets for Tea 9d. Conveyance Tickets to be obtained from Mr. G. W. Harrison, 118, Broad Street.

A little over twelve months after the laying of the foundation stone, on Wednesday 15 July 1903 the opening services of the new church were held. In contrast to the day of the stone laying, the weather was glorious. Rev. Herbert H. Snell conducted a service at 3.30 p.m. and Rev. Ambrose Shepherd gave an eloquent sermon. Before the offering Mr Snell announced that the church still had a debt of £600 and he listed those who had sent money to clear this debt. He read one letter out that had been sent by Mr Leonard Sutton in which he said:

> I have been glad when passing to see that at last an effort has been made to build a place of worship for Spencers Wood, and, although I have no connection with the village or the Congregational Church, I gladly enclose a cheque for £5 as a small contribution to the effort.[17]

1482. Congregational Church, Spencers Wood.

Exterior of the
1903 church

Interior of the
1903 church

After the service tea was provided in the Old Chapel and the Institute and later, at 7 o'clock, a public meeting was held. This time the Mayor of Reading, Mr A. H. Bull, presided over the meeting, and both he and Mr Owen Ridley gave messages of congratulation to the community. Mr Soundy of Trinity Church (who 'was given a very cordial greeting') spoke of the old days and how the chapel started with seventeen children and two women meeting in the afternoon, progressed to an evening service and then a morning service, and congregations of 25 to 40 or 50 people, and 'had grown until it had reached its present strength':

> He said he wished to be assured as to whether he was really, truly, and actually in Spencers Wood Chapel. (Laughter.) It seemed difficult to believe it. As he looked back upon the years that had flown and thought of the congregation that used to assemble in the old-fashioned tumble-down building just outside about 40 years ago, it seemed too good to be true that they were now assembling in that beautiful building. ... That building was to be filled, because where there was one person living within half a mile of the place 42 years ago there were 20 living there now.[18]

Lastly Mr Morris from the architectural firm that designed the church spoke: he congratulated the builder, Mr Edwin Wheeler, and also Mr Dearlove for making the grounds look so good. Finally, Rev. Ambrose Shepherd gave his second address of the day.[19]

A new chapter of the Church thus began in 1903 and from this time we have some records of church meetings. The Church was not autonomous and a Deacon of Trinity Congregational Church in Reading always had to preside over its meetings, whose decisions had to be ratified by Trinity. It was decided at the first meeting that 'members of other Free Churches ... who for various reasons could not see their way clear to sever their connection with those churches, and yet are regularly communicating with us' should be allowed to attend meetings but not to vote. It was with relief that in 1905 the debt on the new building was paid off with the proceeds of a bazaar held at Trinity Church that was organised to help Spencers Wood. At a meeting in October 1907 the question of obtaining a resident Pastor for the church was discussed and 'a memorial [sic] was sent to Trinity Church urging the desirability of such a step'. The meeting pledged to raise £50 p.a. towards his support.[20]

Rev. Albert Swift was appointed Pastor in February 1908, presumably part-time, as he asked the church later that year if they still wanted a resident pastor. The Church Members decided to invite Henry Edward Cole (b. 1871), an Evangelist from Stanford-in-the-Vale, who had been to the Harvest Thanksgiving in 1907, for an interview. In 1907 he had stayed for 10 days, taking Bible Studies and Special Services. He was a native of Woodford, Gloucester, who had been associated with the YMCA at Egham for seven years before serving at Stanford Congregational Church for another seven years.[21]

Initially, as Mr Cole was not a trained minister, they decided to ask him to take a three-year course followed by an examination to become an ordained minister. Unsurprisingly, Mr Cole refused these terms, as he had been educated at the Pastor's College in London (later known as Spurgeon's College), but such was the impression he had made on the members, they called for a vote. Twenty-seven members voted to invite him on his terms and only six were against. Cole accepted the offer and he took his first service as Pastor on the first Sunday in August 1908. He and his wife were accepted into Church Membership in March 1909. He was to become a much-loved Pastor who oversaw the growth of the Church. He led them in the dark days of the First World War and on into the '20s and '30s.[22]

Mr H. E. Cole, Pastor from 1908 to 1933.

In 1929 Trinity Church suggested that the Spencers Wood Church should become self-supporting. Spencers Wood had had much help and guidance from Trinity Church over the years but now was the time to stand on their own feet. It was decided that this would happen gradually over four years. Spencers Wood Church would increase its contribution to Mr Cole's stipend yearly until it was paying all of it.[23] The following year, 1930, Mr Cole celebrated his 21st Anniversary and was presented on this occasion with 'a beautiful wallet containing 21 Treasury notes' (presumably £1 notes). He preached and the Minutes record his success:

> The services were most helpful and everyone felt impressed by the Pastor's earnest and heartfelt addresses and went away refreshed for another year of service to the Master.[24]

In 1933 Pastor Cole sent a letter to the Deacons, regretting that, after 25 years, owing to poor health he was resigning. His resignation was accepted with regret and never again would they have a Pastor with them for so long. He was presented with a cheque for £27 at his last service. Within a few months of his retirement, Pastor Cole had a stroke and he became an invalid. It is recorded in the minutes that 'Pastor H. E. Cole was called to higher service on the 12th September 1936'. His funeral was held at the church and there was a large attendance, as he was greatly loved by all his flock.[25] His obituary in the local paper states that:

> During his ministry at Spencers Wood, Mr Cole was a valued member of the Parish Council. He did good work during the Great War as an organiser of entertainments on behalf of soldiers, especially when the Leicestershire Regiment and the Northumberland Fusiliers were stationed at Swallowfield. As he was too old for military service, Mr Cole worked on the land, at Frank Luckwell's Farm. Both Mr Cole and Mr James Hayes were officially recognised for services rendered during the war. Mr Cole was well known in Reading Non-conformist churches and was an ardent temperance worker.[26]

Meanwhile, in 1934, Rev. John Phillips was appointed Pastor and his Induction Service was held in April of that year. As we have already seen it was at this time the members of the church decided to build a Manse and a building fund and committee were set up. They borrowed £200 (interest-free) from the Congregational Church Building Society, to be paid back in five annual instalments of £40 and the Manse was built in 1935. The photograph of Mr Cole (see p. 65) was paid for by private subscription and placed in the church vestry in 1935.[27]

In 1937, the church celebrated its Centenary as it was believed that the old chapel had been opened in 1837. The members had been working on this

### Snippets from the Minutes

There was annoyance in the village in 1901 about the public house and the sweet shop being open on Sundays.

After discussion in 1903 it was decided to use the church hymnbooks on Sunday mornings and Moody & Sankey hymns in the evening.

The Church had a visit from Rev. Thomas Johnson, a coloured minister and emancipated slave in 1903.

Three Mile Cross Methodists were given permission to hold their Good Friday Services at the Chapel in 1924.

Who would open the fete in 1930? Lady Head was asked but could not do it. So they tried Mrs Allen of Stanbury, then Lady Mowbray and finally Mrs Marcus Adams who agreed to open the fete.

The Institute was let out in 1940 to teachers of the evacuees and to the military for entertaining the troops based locally.

A decision was made in 1953 to install electricity in the Institute and the Manse but not in the Church.

Electricity was installed in the church in 1955.

In 1961, it was reported that there were mice in the church but on inspection they were found to be bats.

In 1966, Mr Owen Ridley's family returned the silver trowel that he used for laying the foundation stone in 1902.

Woodworm was found in the church in 1968/9.

In 1970 the members decided to put the land behind the Institute up for sale. It raised £3,250.

The Centenary of the Congregational Church (1937). Left to right: Leslie Cole (son of Pastor Cole), two visiting ministers (Rev. Frank Ballard and the Rev. W. J. McAdam), Mrs Franklin, Mrs E. Lowe, Rev. John Phillips (minister of church), Mrs Wellstead (secretary of church, her children Margaret and Christine in front), Miss Bentall (from Trinity Congregational Church, Reading), Mrs Tucker (with hands on fence), wife of the Co-op Store Manager, who is perhaps the man holding his hat.

project since 1933 and the event took place on Sunday 6 June and Monday 7 June. Rev. W. J. McAdam spoke at the Sunday services and, on Monday, Rev. Frank Ballard, who had been a Sunday School scholar at the church, took the service at 4 o'clock. Tea was provided in the Institute at 5.15 p.m. and a public meeting was held at 7 o'clock. Mrs Ethel Lowe had written to many one-time worshippers who had moved on for their memories, and three of these letters have proved very helpful in writing this history. The Centenary event resulted in £77 6s. 4d., which was put towards the Manse Building Fund (to help pay off the mortgage).[28]

In 1939 Rev. Phillips announced that he was moving on to be Moderator of the West Midlands Province and, when he took up this post early in 1940, he offered to pay the mortgage on the Manse while he was still living in it. The Church had no minister to replace him and they approached Rev. Hiley, Pastor of Twyford, to oversee their church as well as his own for twelve months and to pay him £40 for the year for the extra work and the transport costs. Mr Hiley continued in this position until 1947 when he retired, and Mr Phillips finally moved out of the Manse. In June, at a special meeting of the Church and Congregation, 'it was realized that, even with a substan[t]ial grant from central funds, the Church could not support a minister' and they passed a resolution 'to release the Manse as a residence for a Home Missioner of the County Union'.[29]

In October Rev. W. E. H. Organe was invited to become Pastor 'at a nominal stipend'. The Church could only afford to fund £40 of his annual stipend, with another £40 being contributed by the County Union, Mr Organe paying the Manse mortgage (£4 0s. 3d.) and the rates. Only two years later, however, he announced that he had decided to retire. The County Union suggested that the Spencers Wood congregation might like to share a minister as they were struggling in the financial area. It was suggested that a minister should be shared between Twyford, Spencers Wood and Pangbourne, but at a meeting on 24 August 1949 (the minutes of which record that there were 32 Church Members), Spencers Wood said they would only consider sharing with one other church and Pangbourne did not agree with the proposed grouping either. Organe finally retired the following March, but it was not until 24 September that a part-time minister, Mr Colin Evans, started his ministry. He stayed until 1953 when he was transferred to Leeds by the Ministry of Supply for whom he worked. Ministers were in short supply and the following suggestions were made: '1. Full time semi-retired man; 2. Part time man; 3. Link up with another Church using our Manse and Church as head quarters; 4. List B man'; the meeting agreed to ask the Moderator if a List B man was available. Meanwhile they had a temporary minister, Mr Hopkins. In the summer of 1955 a new full-time minister, Rev. Graham Whittock moved into the Manse with his wife, a schoolteacher. The same year, electricity was finally installed in the church, at a cost of £57 16s., the Manse and the Institute having been supplied a couple of years earlier.[30]

In 1964, a decree from the County Union said 'no church with less than 60 members could have a full-time minister'. During the '50s and '60s, there was a succession of ministers, none staying more than three years.

## Falling Attendances

In 1949, there had been discussions about amalgamating the Congregational Church and the Presbyterian Church. However, in 1951, it was announced 'that the two churches would work together but stay separate'. Two decades later, in 1972, Spencers Wood Congregational Church joined the union with the Presbyterian Church of England, becoming the Spencers Wood United Reformed Church (URC).[31]

Unfortunately, the numbers attending church services kept falling. In 1969 the Manse (built just over 30 years earlier) was sold for £5,850. The average attendance at services was 17 and there were few young faces among the congregation, but the Church struggled on through the '70s and '80s. In the early '90s, such were the problems of all the churches in the area, with shrinking and aging congregations, that in 1993 all three, the Anglican church of St Michael and All Angels, the United Reformed Church and the Three Mile Cross Methodist Chapel, discussed merging, with the possibility of a single joint church centre (see also Chapter Ten).

In 1994, a Declaration of Intent was drawn up[32] but the Methodist Church Council felt unable to accept this Declaration and the URC concluded that it was not possible to enter the project without the Methodists. However each church expressed a wish to continue working together and to build upon the friendship and co-operation that had developed. To this end they decided to continue with regular Sunday worship together on the first Sunday of the month but to no longer meet for morning worship on the third Sunday of the month. The URC and the Methodists eventually signed a different Declaration of Intent in 2000 (see above).[33]

In 1995, there were discussions with King's, an evangelical church, who wanted to use the Congregational Church for worship: the proposal was to remove the pews at the back of the church 'so that the Kings congregation can use the space … for their (less formal) worship. On the Sunday morning when the URC/Methodist congregation worships at Spencers Wood URC, the Kings congregation will hold family worship in the church hall. The Kings Church are very sensitive to the feelings of the URC congregation'.[34]

The two non-conformist churches continued to meet regularly together in one of the two churches. But by 1998, the membership had further decreased with seven URC members, all elderly, and eighteen Methodist members, again all elderly (including four car-drivers of whom two were over eighty). The churches were having separate church meetings, and their finances were separate, but the whole of the congregation would meet to consider matters of policy in the life of the church. A decision was made that, on amalgamation, they would meet at Three Mile Cross as the Methodist church was in better order that the United Reformed Church. It had been hoped that the latter could be developed into a Community Centre but this did not happen, and in May 1999, Spencers Wood United Reformed Church resolved that the redundant church buildings at Spencers Wood, 'together with the land are no longer required for their intended purpose and therefore instruct the Wessex Trust to dispose of the property'. The buildings and land were sold to a property company, which converted the church very tastefully into apartments and built houses to the rear of it.[35]

The new joint church was to be known as Three Mile Cross United Church. The first minister of the joint Church was Rev. Terry Hinks and it was expected that the ministry would be an alternating one, with Terry being followed by a

Methodist minister. There were special services and celebrations in July 2000 at Three Mile Cross in the open air to commemorate the signing of the new constitution and the 125th Anniversary of the Methodist Chapel. The signed copy of the constitution is in the Berkshire Record Office.[36]

## Notes

[1] BRO, D/N 44/6/2/1/1, Memo, 1824.

[2] BRO, D/N 44/9/3/1, Certificate of registration of the building as a place of worship, 1817.

[3] W. H. Summers, *History of the Congregational churches in the Berks, South Oxon and South Bucks Association, with notes on the earlier nonconformist history of the district* (1905), p. 197; BRO, D/N 44/6/2/1/6; for example, the typescript in the possession of SWLHG, 'Reminiscences of Spencers Wood Old Chapel' by Mrs E. Lowe (1937), begins 'The old Chapel was built in the year 1837...'. Mrs Lowe also mentions that 'A tree was given by a Mrs Simmonds in memory of her husband, which was planted in the grounds, and I am told it is over 100 yers old, and we ought to value it very much. (note may have been planted 1837)'.

[4] Photocopy of manuscript, 'Recollections of Old Sunday School Days at Spencers Wood', by Jack Povey (1937), in possession of SWLHG. Jack lived in Spencers Wood for four years around 1893 and left when he was 11.

[5] 'Reminiscences' by Mrs E. Lowe.

[6] BRO, D/N 44/1/2/1, Church meeting minutes, 1923–56, 9 Jan., 20 Feb., 25 Apr. 1934.

[7] D/N 44/1/2/1, 20 Dec. 1934.

[8] *Reading Mercury*, 31 Mar. 1894.

[9] *Berkshire Chronicle*, 25 Mar. 1899; BRO D/N 10/14/17, Scrapbook, cutting from the *Christian Commonwealth*, 1 Oct. 1901.

[10] D/N 10/14/17, cutting from the *Christian Commonwealth*, 1 Oct. 1901.

[11] D/N 10/14/17, cutting from the *Reading Observer* (annotated '2 May 1902').

[12] D/N 10/14/17, undated newspaper cutting, 'Spencers Wood'.

[13] *Reading Standard*, 12 July 1902.

[14] Ibid.

[15] Ibid.

[16] *Reading Standard*, 18 July 1903, presumably taken from Architect's specification.

[17] Ibid.

[18] Ibid.

[19] Ibid; see Chapter Eight for more of Wheeler's building work.

[20] BRO D/N 10/1/1/1, Records of the Congregational Church assembling at Spencers Wood, Church Minutes, 28 Feb. 1901, 19 Oct. 1905, 25 Oct. 1907.

[21] D/N 10/1/1/1, 22 Apr. 1908, 24 Sept. 1907, 3 June 1908; D/N 10/14/17, undated newspaper cutting, 'Death of Rev. H. E. Cole'.

[22] 'Death of Rev. H. E. Cole'; D/N 10/1/1/1, 3 June 1908, 7 June 1908, 2 Mar. 1909.

[23] Church meeting minutes, 10 Dec. 1929.

[24] D/N 44/1/2/1, 16–17 Feb. 1930.

[25] 'Death of Rev. H. E. Cole'; D/N 44/1/2/1, 18 Apr. 1933, 5 Nov. 1936.

[26] 'Death of Rev. H. E. Cole'.

[27] D/N 44/1/2/1, 25 Apr. 1934, 21 Feb. and 15 Oct. 1935. They received a further loan from Mr Edgar Ridley of Reading of £100 repayable over 5 years at 4.5%. We know from the minutes that building started in 1935 but there is no record of it finishing.

[28] D/N 44/1/2/1, 28 Mar. 1933, 8 Mar. 1934, 22 June 1937.

[29] D/N 44/1/2/1, 4 Aug. 1939, 18 Jan. 1940, 11 July 1940 ('An application had been made by the Baptist Union to take over the Spencers Wood Church and work it with their own district churches; this offer had of course been refused by the Union and a suggestion had been made that Rev. H. G. Hiley of Twyford be asked to undertake the oversight of Spencers Wood in addition his church at Twyford...'), 4 June 1947.

[30] D/N 44/1/2/1, 8 Oct. 1947, 1923–56, p. 195, 27 July 1949, 24 Aug., 28 Sept. 1949, 6 Sept., 27 Sept. 1950, 8 July 1953, 8 Oct. 1953, 10 Feb. and 7 Sept. 1955.

[31] A commemorative tablet now in the possession of Spencers Wood Local History Group says, 'This tablet is erected in thanksgiving to God for the formation of the United Reformed Church in England and Wales on 5th October 1972 during the ministry here of Pastor Louis Steer'.

[32] BRO, D/N 44/13/1, Papers relating to proposals for joint working with, and towards eventual union with, Three Mile Cross Methodist Church, Declaration of Intent, Oct. 1994.

[33] Declaration of Intent, 2000, copy in possession of SWLHG.

[34] D/N 44/13/1, Memo from Terry Hinks, 15 June 1995.

[35] Sales literature in the possession of SWLHG.

[36] D/N 44/13/1, Three Mile Cross Methodist Church and Spencers Wood United Reformed Church: A local ecumenical partnership: Constitution, signed and dated 1 July 2001.

## CHAPTER SIX

# Stanbury

*Margaret Bampton*

I n the years around 1860 F. W. Allfrey built a house – now long gone – called Stanbury. Allfrey (1819–1915) was from a commercial and brewing family.[1] His father Edward Allfrey (1770–1834) came from a Sussex yeoman background but made his career first in shipping insurance at Lloyds and then invested as a partner in Reid and Co. of the Griffin Brewery in Clerkenwell. Edward Allfrey established an estate around Salebury and Robertbridge in Sussex but left his four sons enough for them all to acquire country estates. The eldest son, Robert (1809–75) bought Wokefield House, not far from Spencers Wood. The second son, H. W. Allfrey, bought Hemingford House at Alveston in Warwickshire. The youngest son inherited his father's Sussex estate. Frederick William, the third son, built a house which was far more modest in scale than Wokefield, but he also created a landscape. The house has gone, but much of Allfrey's landscape remains.

The Stanbury estate was, in effect, the land of Hill House Farm. Hill House had been sold several times in the first half of the nineteenth century: in 1815, then in 1833 and again in 1842.[2] When Allfrey bought it is not clear, but it may have been in 1855 when in quick succession the farm tenant had a farm sale of his dead and live stock (a sign that he was quitting the farm) and then at the end of April there was a sale of standing timber on the premises (which may indicate that the farm was in process of being sold). But no sale notice has been found, and it is possible that the sale was made by private treaty. We can suggest at least three reasons why Allfrey might have been attracted to the Hill House estate. The first was proximity to his elder brother at Wokefield. The second was that Hill House itself was considered to be a good house and suitable for a gentleman and his family until his mansion was built. When he was nominated to be sheriff of Berkshire in 1860, his address was given as Hill House, Shinfield.[3] (By the time of the 1861 census, he was of 'Stanbury house'). The third was that the farm contained a suitable site for a new, big house, with room for gardens and pleasure grounds and extensive views over the neighbouring countryside. Additional land was added to this by the enclosure of the common, in which

*Opposite:*
Aerial view
of Stanbury,
Spencers Wood,
12 August 1931
[EPW036203 ©
Historic England]

Stanbury: the mansion before and after the fire of 1960

Allfrey may have been a prime mover, as we saw in Chapter One.

In 1874, Allfrey purchased more land to the south of the lodge and built two cottages nearby called Ivy Cottages, plus a house called Oak Lodge, opposite, on the corner of The Square (see Chapter Eight), to house his employees. The estate of just over 100 acres was bounded by the Highlands estate to the south, Grazeley Road to the north and Woodcock Lane to the west, although there were one or two old cottages, and the site of Three Mile Cross Chapel, that Frederick Allfrey did not own. In 1889, he purchased the land where the current Library stands. There he built and maintained the Infants' School and its school house, until the school closed in 1915. Mr Allfrey was not ostentatious but he was very charitable. He was a churchwarden at Grazeley Church and, when he died in 1915, his cortège was taken from his home over footpaths to Grazeley, where he was buried. Frederick's daughter, Louisa, married her cousin, Mortimer Allfrey, the son of Robert, Frederick's brother and they lived at Farley Castle. Robert lived at Wokefield Park and he, Mortimer and Louisa are all buried in Grazeley church graveyard.[4]

When auctioned in 1919, the mansion had many rooms, including 17 bedrooms, and some ground-floor rooms had central heating. Hill House was still part of the estate, as were four cottages for Allfrey's staff. The entrance lodge to the estate, now called the South Lodge, was at the end of the Wellingtonia Avenue, which was gated.[5]

## Stanbury Estate Details from the 1919 sale particulars

When Stanbury was auctioned in 1919 by Nicholas of Reading, the estate (158 acres in all) included the mansion with 100 acres of parkland, stabling, lodge, farmery, eight cottages, the village school and school house, Hill House, Oak Lodge and several lots of undeveloped land.

**Stanbury** had a tiled hall, morning room, drawing room, dining room, library, gun room, servants' hall, housekeeper's room, larder, servants' sitting room, kitchen, pantry, two sculleries and a butler's pantry with an adjoining bedroom. The principal staircase led to eleven bedrooms, the largest of which was 26 ft by 17 ft 9 in., with 'views extending to Burghfield Hill, the Chiltern Hills, etc'. On the first floor there were also a billiard room (29ft by 18ft 9in.) and a smoking room (16ft by 12ft). On the second floor were six bedrooms, all with 'excellent fireplaces'. The house had 'extensive cellarage' and outside there were two 'closets for servants', coal and coke houses, larder, dairy, 'man's room' and other buildings.

The water supply was described as 'never failing, from springs by force pumps' and there were 'large soft water tanks', but water and gas mains 'could be laid on to the house if desired'. The drainage had 'an excellent fall at a considerable distance from the house'.

**The stables** contained seven loose boxes with hay-lofts over, harness room and standing for four horses. There were large double and single garages used as a coach house.

**The farmery** consisted of 'nag stabling of two boxes', two stalls, a saddle room and meal house. There were a 'cowhouse for 8, bullhouse, piggeries and poultry houses'. Further buildings included '3 loose summering boxes and trap house, large corrugated iron carriage house, 9 timber and corrugated iron loose boxes, meal and corn store and loft'.

**The cottages** included 'a pair of modern brick and tiled cottages near the stables'; the 'Picturesque Entrance Lodge'; Weather Cock Cottages, described as 'a picturesque 18th century block of 3 cottages'; finally there was a 'superior brick and tiled cottage'.

**The 'beautiful old pleasure grounds'** were described as 'grandly timbered'. As well as the Wellingtonia carriage drive, lawns, gardens, conservatory and azalea house, they included a 'beautiful continuous yew hedge about 100 yards in length broken in one part by a yew harbour', walled fruit garden, vegetable garden, orchards and vinery.

**Hill House** consisted of a spacious entrance hall, drawing room, dining room, kitchen, pantry, larder and scullery. Between the ground and first floors were a bathroom and WC. On the first floor were a lounge and four bedrooms. The second floor had another four bedrooms. Outside were a garage, covered washing yard, poultry house, granary and other outbuildings. It had over 5 acres of land attached, described as 'delightful old pleasure grounds'.

**Oak Lodge**, opposite the entrance lodge, was described as an 'attractive creeper-clad, brick and tiled residence', had an entrance hall, drawing room, dining room, kitchen, larder, three bedrooms, large bathroom and pretty gardens (see p. 108).

**The school** was described as 'a very large lofty building' with a large private room, lavatory, bathroom, cloakroom, lobby and a large garden. The adjoining **school house** had a large sitting room, kitchen, scullery with a pump, and three large bedrooms. Outside were coal-houses and a yard containing a WC and EC (earth closets). (The closets are still there. See Chapter Nine for more about the school.)

Between the school house and the entrance lodge there were another pair of 'tiled, creeper-clad' cottages (known later as **Ivy Cottages**): one had two bedrooms, the other three, both had living room, kitchen, coal-house and EC.

'The Old Stables' at Stanbury, from a sale catalogue of 1975 (*right*); 'The Coach House' at Stanbury in 1985 (*below*)

In 1920, the whole estate was sold to Charles Allen and he probably built the North Lodge opposite St Michael's Church. During this time the annual show of the Swallowfield, Grazeley and Spencers Wood Horticultural Society was sometimes held at Stanbury. The Allens were keen on hunting and the South Berkshire Hunt often met there. Mr Allen died in 1931 but two of his daughters continued to live in the mansion. Mr and Mrs Allen and one daughter were buried at Grazeley Church.

Between the death of Mr Allen and the start of the Second World War, there is little information available about Stanbury and its grounds except that the government requisitioned the mansion on behalf of the Army, paying compensation of £300 p.a., and Nissen huts lined the Wellingtonia Avenue and the side of the mansion house, surrounded by barbed wire (see Chapter Thirteen).[6]

In 1943 Ernest Judd (of Judd's Sawmills), 'Haulage Contractor', purchased part of the dilapidated estate, and he sold South Lodge in 1953.[7] Two years later, in 1945, much of the remainder of the estate – excluding Hill House, Pursers Farm, Ivy Cottages (which had been sold by the Allen family in 1942), Oak Lodge and Weathercock Cottages – was auctioned, but the Army continued to use the house for some years after the war ended. North Lodge, a modern bungalow with 25 acres let to Mr Norris, was lot number four.[8] In 1949, the bailiff's house, Oak Lodge, was sold as a 'pleasant detached residence' with an 'attractive well timbered garden'.[9] After the war, the Nissen huts were used to house homeless people, but were mostly demolished in the 1950s by the local haulage firm of Hadleys in Hyde End Road. (This firm was started in the 1930s by Ernest Hadley and continued by his nephew, Alan, whose company built eight houses in Hyde End Road using the concrete blocks that they produced.[10])

In the 1950s, the then owner of Stanbury, Reading estate agent Robert Moffat, purchased a large conservatory (60 ft by 20 ft), known as the 'orangery', from the Maiden Erleigh (Reading) estate of Sol Joel, a South African diamond millionaire, who had had it built in 1902. Moffat pieced together the 2000 pieces of conservatory 'like a gigantic jigsaw of wood and metal', fixed the 1700 panes of glass with 'a ton of putty', and erected it near the house to the north of the stables, which he called 'Stanbury Park'. He then used it for charitable fund-raising events such as receptions and cocktail parties. Stanbury itself was sold to a developer to convert into flats, but a fire in 1960 meant that it had to be demolished. In 1969–70 a residential development known as Wellington Court was built on the site, approached by a private road, and in later years more houses have been built nearby.

In 1976, Moffat put his house, the orangery and 32 acres of grounds on the market, and the following year they were bought for £100,000 by Khan Lari, an 'Arab businessman' who planned to spend a further £100,000 on enlarging the house. By 1983, however, 'Stanbury Park' was in the hands of David and Patti Stevens who wanted to sell the house and were trying to sell the orangery separately. The stumbling block was the high price – quoted as £13,000 – of dismantling and rebuilding it. Eventually, however, it was sold to a buyer who moved it to Cornwall.'[11]

The stable block and farmery complex were also converted into accommodation (see opposite) and are currently inhabited, as are the two lodges, North Lodge having been extended in 2015–16.

## Notes

[1] For the family, see the account by Nicholas Kingsley at landedfamilies.blogspot.co.uk/2014/02/106-allfrey-of-wokefield-park.html.

[2] BRO D/EX 303/E1/1, Sales Particulars, 1815; *Reading Mercury,* 15 July 1833; *Berkshire Chronicle,* 7 May 1842.

[3] *Berkshire Chronicle,* 17 Nov. 1860.

[4] Barbara Debney, 'Stanbury', in *Our Village of Spencers Wood* (Spencers Wood Local History Group, 2001), pp. 88–94.

[5] Reading Local Studies Library, Nicholas of Reading, 1919, 'Stanbury Estate Sales Particulars'.

[6] BRO, D/ENS B/20/2, 'Stanbury' (Nicholas, 1945).

[7] BRO, D/EX 1342/14 Deeds of property including Stanbury Estate Plans, deed of conveyance between Walter Augustus Allen, Violet Hilda Allen and Elizabeth Mary Snelus Allen, and Harold Judd, Haulage Contractor, 22 Mar. 1943.

[8] D/ENS B/20/2.

[9] BRO, D/ENS B/24/59, 'Oak Lodge, The Square' (Nicholas, 1949).

[10] *Memories of Reading* (North Books Ltd, 1999).

[11] *Reading Evening Post,* 28 July 1976, 11 Jan. 1977, 30 Sept. 1983.

## CHAPTER SEVEN

# The Post Office

*Patricia Green*

A brief updated version of Sheila Davis, 'The Post Office, 1885–1993' in *Our Village of Spencers Wood* (Spencers Wood Local History Group, 2001), pp. 76–81.

The first Post and Telegraph Office was established in 1885. Eventually postal deliveries from Spencers Wood included Swallowfield, Riseley, Three Mile Cross and Grazeley, and the service was run from a room in the front of a house on Basingstoke Road. The postcard opposite shows Basingstoke Road with the Post Office on the left of the picture. This house, though now considerably altered, continues to be the Post Office and the home of the sub-postmaster. A manual telephone exchange was added to the Post Office later, and this was handled at Spencers Wood until the Reading exchange was automated in 1934.

The first Postmaster was John Lowe, who was also a general dealer and made deliveries with his pony and trap. He was assisted by his wife, Mary, who is described in the 1901 census as 'Post Mistress' while he is a 'Coal Merchant'; they had a 15-year-old son, Wilfred, 'Letter Deliverer'. In 1911, Ivy Wheeler, their niece, was 'Post Office Assistant': Mary was the sister-in-law of William Wheeler (see Chapter Eight), father of Ivy. The business passed to the eldest son of Mary and John Lowe, Gilbert, whose wife Ethel was very much involved in the Congregational Church Centenary celebrations in 1937. Ethel's daughter Olive, who married Cyril Franklin (see Chapter Five), and the Franklins ran it until 1968. Mr Rickaby bought it in 1969, and then in 1971 sold it again to Tony and Sheila Davis. As the village grew, so the Post Office became busier. It dealt with many changes in the way the General Post Office organised the national service. In the early 1980s, Tony acquired a Sinclair computer and wrote a program to facilitate producing the weekly Post Office balance. He wrote articles about this in *The Sub-Postmaster, the Official Journal of the National Federation of Sub-Postmasters*, receiving more than 200 letters of interest and selling copies of the program to fellow sub-postmasters. It was many years before the General Post Office itself computerised the offices.

The delivery of mail across the five villages was mostly made by a team of postmen on bicycles or using the two vans. The men were based at the sorting office beside the house, where the letters and parcels were brought

Basingstoke
Road, Spencers
Wood, looking
south. The Post
Office is to the
left, and the
sign-board of
the Red Lion
Inn and the
corner of Beech
Hill Road are
to the right.
1900–1909:
postcard from
P. J. Drinkwater,
of the County
Branch Library,
The Mitford,
Three Mile
Cross, to the
County Librarian,
Abbey Street,
Reading.

between 4.30 and 5.00 a.m., six mornings a week. Sheila and Tony retired in 1993, having coped with decimalisation, privatisation and the separation of telephone and postal businesses, and the cost and trading implications of the new National Business Rating. They built a new house, Dorneycroft, on the site of the old sorting office.

The Post Office
(1950s or '60s).

The Post Office just after it was transformed into a general store in November 2015. Dorneycroft can be seen to the right

The Post Office was then run by Barry and Joyce Duxbury, who had previously run a general store (Harrisons) on Basingstoke Road. The sorting office and local delivery of mail ceased at this time. Elaine Harris and her family then bought the business and moved into the house. After eight years the Post Office was sold on again to Arjun Odedra. The functions of the Post Office have changed over the years, but it has remained a useful and significant part of village life.

At the end of 2015, the Post Office underwent radical change. Due to a change in Post Office policy, the Postmaster was obliged to enlarge the store and take on a One Stop shop franchise in order to meet Post Office requirements. The new-look Post Office opened for business at the end of November 2015 and seems to be a great success.

## CHAPTER EIGHT

# A Walk around The Square

*Jackie Blow and Jeannie Brice*

As you can see from the diagram below, The Square is shaped as a parallelogram, rather than a square – as it follows the pre-existing field boundaries. We are taking you on a walk around that parallelogram, starting opposite Spencers Wood Library, outside Whiteknights estate agents. We first go north along Basingstoke Road and then turn right into The Square proper, looking at the houses on the right-hand side of the road. At the end of The Square we turn right into Hyde End Road, go up as far as the back of Whiteknights, and then turn back on ourselves, returning to The Square itself, this time going in the opposite direction, looking at the other side of the road. Along the way we tell you about all the interesting things we have discovered (historical or not!)[1] We finish at the top end of The Square on Basingstoke Road.

Route of the walk around The Square

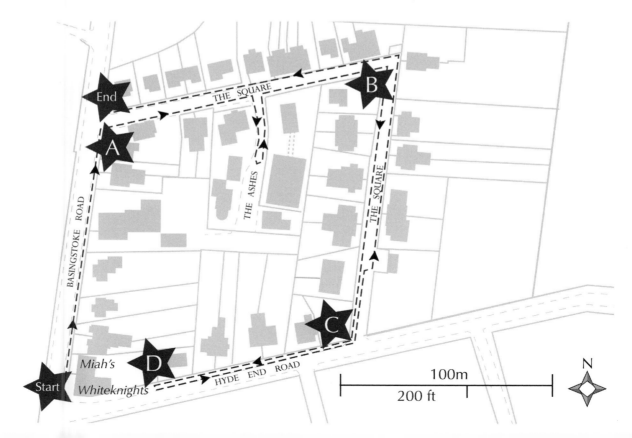

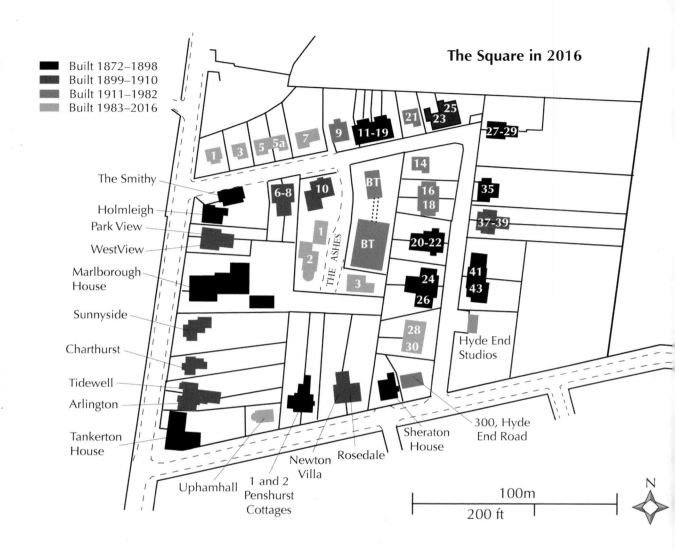

The Square in 2016

**Built 1872–1898**
**Built 1899–1910**
**Built 1911–1982**
**Built 1983–2016**

The Smithy
Holmleigh
Park View
WestView
Marlborough House
Sunnyside
Charthurst
Tidewell
Arlington
Tankerton House

Uphamhall
1 and 2 Penshurst Cottages
Newton Villa
Rosedale
Sheraton House
300, Hyde End Road

THE ASHES
BT
BT
Hyde End Studios

100m
200 ft

N

## House Names in The Square

6 Brantham
8 Bergholt
10 Ash Cottage (formerly Ash)
11, 15, 17, 19 (formerly 1–4, Rose Cottages)
14 Chalfont Mead (formerly Casseldene)
16 Jesmond
20 Fairhaven (formerly Roselea)

22 Wilcot
23 Wisteria
25 Syringa (formerly Casseldene)
24 St Hilda
26 Dilwyn (formerly Summeda, then Sunnyside)
27 New Home
29 Alverne (formerly Windmill Cottage)

35 Hawthorne
37 Laburnum
39 Hope Cottage
41–43 Stanley Villas (formerly 1–2, Stanley Cottages)

Aerial view of
The Square,
12 August 1931
[EPW036202
© Historic England]

But first, a bit of history... On the 1872 Ordnance Survey 1:2500 map of Spencers Wood, the area now covered by The Square and bounded by Basingstoke Road in the west and Hyde End Road to the south was just a field (see p. 9, bottom left). By 1899 when the map was next revised, it showed that five detached houses, five pairs of semi-detached houses, and one row of four cottages, as well as the smithy, had been completed (nineteen homes in all). A plot was marked out for a further pair of semis. The section running down from Basingstoke Road was initially called 'New Road', and the piece running to Hyde End Road was called 'Headley Road'. Twelve years later in 1911 the second revision of the map showed that six more pairs of semis had been completed, and four detached houses (bringing the total to 35 dwellings). Further development was fairly sporadic over the next 80-odd years, with only seven houses being added over the period 1911–93. Since then there have been eleven new houses built and two demolished; and Tankerton House has been doubled in size. There are now over 50 residences (of which two also house an estate agent and a restaurant), as well as the old smithy building, a telephone exchange and the currently vacant, enlarged premises at Marlborough House.

On to the walk... Let's start on the corner of Hyde End Road and Basingstoke Road. This is **Tankerton House**, which in the early days was *Middleton Stores*. The census of 1901 tells us that the stores were run by Robert Jolly Middleton with his family: his wife, Annie, and five boys. Sadly, in 1897, a fire had broken out in the shed at the back of the shop, killing another son, Rupert George, who was only two. By 1911 Robert had extended his family to six boys and two girls, and moved to Grovelands Farm. On the 1911 census Ben Keene was manager, and the shop was called *The Stores*. Then, from 1914 to 1956 the Lee family ran a grocery store here: Mr Alexander Richard Lee died in 1949 and his daughter, Madeline, continued to run the shop until

Tankerton House

Miah's and Whiteknights
in 2016

around 1956. It then became a *Wavy Line* grocery, rented and run by Simon and Molly Curruthurs.

In 1978, Karen Cottee rented the shop, running a florist's and pet food shop and calling it *The Flower Corner*. She went on to buy the shop in 1980, building an extension to the left in 1984/5, and another one at the back two years later. The extension side was rented to *Televid Traders* until they left in 2000, when she sold the whole building to *Miah's* Indian restaurant, who continued to rent out the original piece to *Whiteknights* estate agents. In 2016 both businesses are still operating from these premises. The extension has recently had two dormer windows added to match the dormer windows in the original Tankerton House.

As we walk north (in the direction of Reading) along Basingstoke Rd, leaving Miah's behind us, we pass on the right two semi-detached houses, **Arlington** and then **Tidewell**. Arlington was once lived in by the Cleave family,

Tidewell and
Arlington

85

whose daughter married Herbert Horwood. Herbert and his father, William, were the last bakers at the *Old Bakery* (further south along Basingstoke Road). The *Old Bakery* has had many other uses since World War II, more recently a hairdressers (*Anita's*), and now a hair and beauty salon called *Blissimi*. Tidewell was where the Rogers family lived: Mr Rogers had three daughters, only one of whom (Violet) married. One of the Misses Rogers (Dorothy) ran the Little Sunbeams private infants' school here. Mr Rogers was the organist for many years at Farley Hill Church and at least one of his daughters (Daisy) gave music lessons. They were a very musical family and residents often talk of being taught to play the piano by Miss Rogers.

Across the road from Arlington and Tidewell you can see the Library, which you can read all about in Chapter Nine. Continuing along the Basingstoke Road we pass two detached houses, **Charthurst** and **Sunnyside**. Rev. Cole, Pastor of the Congregational Church from 1907 to 1933, lived with his family at Charthurst from at least 1911 to his death in 1936. Sunnyside was originally known as 'Shottesbrooke' and is believed to have been built around 1901. The first resident was a Wilfred Kernutt, a watchmaker, who had a jeweller's shop in London Street, Reading. The Young family rented the house in the 1950s until buying it in 1960, living here for well over 60 years. Gordon Young was a leader in the Boy Scout movement for many years. The present owners bought Sunnyside in 2010.

Charthurst

Sunnyside

Until 1912 **Marlborough House** was a plant nursery and landscape business owned by the Dearlove family. After that, it became a small confectionery shop run by a Miss Horwood (no relation to the previously mentioned Horwoods), until 1921, when it was modernised and made into a much larger Co-op Grocery and Provision store, a branch of the *Reading Co-operative Society*. This was greatly missed when it closed in about 1985. After the Co-op was closed, *Delby's Refrigeration Company* had their offices there before moving to Worton Grange, Reading. More recently the *Society for General Microbiology* operated from it until they moved out in 2013, when the building was put up for auction. At the time of writing, a planning application to convert the building into flats is under consideration.

Dearlove's nursery (*above*) and Marlborough House in 2015 (*left*)

Westview and Parkview in the early twentieth century (*above*) and in 2016 (*below*)

Continuing towards the junction with The Square, we pass the semi-detached houses **Westview** and **Parkview**. Westview is now the location of *Kiddiwinks Childminding*, but before the Second World War Percy Double lived here with his family, while his brother Charles lived in Parkview, with his family. They were the sons of Charles Samuel Strutt Double (1866–1946), who had moved to Berkshire from Suffolk, taking up residence in Spencers Wood some time between 1891 and 1901. He was the farrier, or blacksmith, and in the early 1900s he purchased enough land to build four houses: Westview and

Holmleigh

C. S. Double at work in the smithy (*Farmers' Weekly*, 1938)

Parkview and another pair actually in The Square, Brantham and Bergholt, which were named after villages in Suffolk from which his family had originated. Charles Double senior's house, Holmleigh, was on Basingstoke Road but the smithy and cycle repair business was round the corner in The Square. This led to the area around being known locally as *Doubles' Corner*.[2] Later, the Hyde family lived at Westview, where Marion Pyke (née Hyde) was born in 1941: we will meet her again in a moment.

**Holmleigh** is the last private house on the corner of Basingstoke Road and The Square. Initially Charles and Ellen Double lived there, next door to the smithy. In the 1920s Charles was joined in the business by two of his five sons, Percy and Charles, whom we have already met. The eldest son was killed in the First World War, and the youngest two moved to Cowley, Oxfordshire, to work at the Morris Car Works. Tim Double (grandson of Percy) still runs the garage business in the village today, now located near the corner of Beech Hill Road and Basingstoke Road.

**A** As you turn into The Square, on your left you will see the building that used to be the **Smithy**. It now looks like a garage, and is used for private events and for storage, but originally this was a very active farrier's business, where horses were shod and bicycles mended. Later when cars took over from horses and bicycles, Doubles moved the business to the corner of Basingstoke Road and Beech Hill Road. After this, from approximately 1964 to 1974, the smithy building housed *F. D. Lamb & Son*, a machine parts supplier, which became from 1975 to 1997, *Hycon Hydraulics,* and from then until 2007 sold *Bayer's* bird seed. Its heyday, however, was when it was a farrier's with its fascination for children.

The blacksmith or farrier heated up the metal in a hearth known as a 'forge', and bashed it into shape on an 'anvil'; his workplace would have been known as the 'smithy', or as the 'forge'. By the late nineteenth century many blacksmiths and farriers were diversifying into mending bicycles and eventually would go on to mend cars and supply petrol. You can hear Marion Pyke talking about her memories on our Web site (swlhg.co.uk). She talks of going to the blacksmith's and begging to be allowed to sit on the horse: 'I used to spend a lot of my childhood hanging over the blacksmith's door watching Charlie Double shoe the horses, saying, "Please let me get on the horse, Mr Double"'. Like her mother, Frona, before her, Marion went to Lambs Lane School. The family then moved to a tied cottage on Swallowfield Estate, where her father, Carol, was a mechanic

The old smithy decorated with flags for the Queen's Diamond Jubilee, 4 May 2012

to Sir Arthur Russell. Many people who grew up in and around The Square have given us memories, and the farrier's is very strong in their recollection – among them, John Tonkin. John was an evacuee during the war, and on Saturday mornings watched the farrier 'shoeing the horses, and would pump the bellows for him to keep the forge going'. The words 'farrier' and 'blacksmith' are now used interchangeably but historically a farrier would shoe horses full-time, whereas a blacksmith would be making or repairing tools such as spades or ploughshares, and other objects from nails and hinges to gates and railings.

Many residents, as children, would peer over the door of the smithy in the hope of catching a shire horse being shod. Vic Earley was another one. Vic lived at number 37 when he was a young boy, and he recalls:

> Should I hear that most beautiful rhythmical clang of hammer-on-anvil whilst walking in The Square I would run as fast as my young legs would carry me to the smithy's door. Always this dash made to that door was in hope and with anticipation of his shoeing a great shire horse.

We know that members of the Wheeler family were already living in Spencers Wood in 1871 – initially at the Swallowfield end – describing themselves in the census as builders and bricklayers. The Wheelers had come from Sonning and set up a building business here in Spencers Wood. Edwin Wheeler, bricklayer and builder, was 28 in 1871 and had his 17-year-old brother Frederick, 'his labourer', and a carpenter, George Lane, living with him. Another brother, William Henry Wheeler, a 25-year-old bricklayer, was also living here. We do not know exactly when they built the first houses in The Square, but an indenture dated 5 March 1887 tells us that William purchased three acres of land from Richard Bernard Body for £320. The upside-down L-shaped plot extended from the allotments in the north to Hyde End Road in the south. It covered the area now occupied by odd-numbered houses 1–43 (excluding the eastern parts of the gardens of 29–39), Headley Cottages in Hyde End Road, even-numbered houses 14–26, Sheraton House and 300 Hyde End Road. William sold a parcel of land to his builder brother Edwin, who proceeded to build houses. Like most families of that time the Wheeler family were involved in church life and, when the tin institute at the Congregational Church was destroyed by fire in the 1890s and the young men of the bible class all helped to build a much larger one, this included the three Wheeler boys, William, Owen and Lionel, the sons of William (see the photo of the commemorative tablet on p. 60). Their father, and their uncle, Edwin, were among the many people who donated materials for the project. Tragedy came to the family when in early 1896 seven-year-old Lily, daughter of William, ate red berries from the hedgerow and died.[3]

When the new Congregational Church was built in 1903, the builder was Edwin Wheeler, and one of the first marriages solemnised there was that of Miss Daisy Wheeler, a Sunday School teacher and daughter of William.[4] Being early members of the church, when Edwin's wife died in 1909 he presented a new organ to the church in her memory.[5] Edwin Wheeler's will confirms that he died on 31 December 1912. He left his assets in equal shares to his nine siblings and Charles Aldridge, the nephew of his late wife, Ann.[6] He and his wife did not have any children, so if his brother or sister had pre-deceased him a ninth share was to be distributed between the children of that sibling.

Looking down The Square: Oak Lodge is visible on the left (compare with the photo on p. 109)

You should now have turned off Basingstoke road and into The Square itself! As we continue our walk you will hear more about the Wheeler Family, and their contribution to The Square's history.

On your right you will see examples of the first houses built, in about 1907: the semi-detached **Brantham** and **Bergholt**. We think that these houses were built by William Wheeler for the Double family. Brantham's deeds show that in 1989 they sold a section of their rear garden to *Delby's* for parking, for the sum of £2,000. Three generations of one family occupied Bergholt from 1912 to 2008: George and Rosalie Lake, then their daughter, Rona, who married Ronald Redsell, and finally her son David Redsell.

It's relevant to note that numbering did not come to The Square until 1968. There is a letter dated 25 March 1968 from Wokingham Rural District Council, retained in the deeds of Brantham, confirming 'number 6' for Brantham. On numbering the road, the Council, superstitiously omitted number 13 and also left out numbers 2, 4, 31 and 33, perhaps thinking that enough land was left

for future property development. As you walk around, notice these spaces, and see what you think.

We then approach a detached property, originally called 'Ash', but now called **Ash Cottage**. Look at the bricks carefully: it was built about 1902 and originally had a larger plot with an apple orchard. The first occupant of Ash was John Salter; it was then purchased by James Hayes and his wife. A later resident recalled her mother buying windfall apples from Mrs Hayes. In 1937 part of its

Ash Cottage

orchard was sold to the GPO for their telephone exchange. In 1951, Ash was purchased by Mr and Mrs Leonard Benham for the sum of £2,700 and their conveyance and stamp duty costs were £110 12*s*. 6*d*. Mr Benham had previously run a coal business called *Woods Yard* in Riseley, continuing to run this, and his haulage company, in the yard behind the house. On the retirement of his father, Francis Benham took over the business. In 1998 Francis retired and the house and yard were sold to developers, who built a new cul-de-sac named 'The Ashes', just past Ash Cottage on the right hand side.

The Ashes

Jackie and Chris Blow purchased the house itself and moved in during August 1999. They had rather a large job on their hands to begin with as the house had been used for storage and carpentry work for the building of the three houses in The Ashes. The house had been unoccupied for over a year and the garden had become totally overgrown. They added a bedroom and built the garage. They had always loved the character of this house, never dreaming that one day they would actually live there, and when the time comes to down-size they will be sad to leave.

As you go around the corner you enter **The Ashes**. There are three detached houses, built in 1998, in what used to be Benham's haulage yard. Two have been sold a number of times and one is still lived in by the original owner. As you double-back on yourself, you can see the telephone exchange (now BT) on your right. Vic Earley describes this as having a 'mystique': as boys, he and his friends trespassed anywhere and everywhere, but never on the telephone exchange, because as he recalled, 'something

that worked automatically was rather an anathema to us simple country folk, one might get radiated or electrified or something even worse.'

In December 2000 Wokingham District Council wrote to all residents in The Square to advise them of an application received from a mobile telephone company that wanted to install a phone mast in The Square, a monopole tower, 12.5 metres high. Many people in the street got together to object to this application in what we can only describe as an act of 'people power'.

The telephone exchange

They approached the *Reading Evening Post*, and the *Reading Chronicle* to come and take pictures of their group under the campaign title, 'Just Say No'. Many of them cited dangers to the health of children through microwave radiation. The Square is designated as an area of special interest, and the mast, the residents said, would clearly be out of place with the Victorian and Edwardian homes. A petition was put together with more than 250 signatures and handed to the council. A letter to the mobile phone company was also sent, asking why other less sensitive sites were not chosen, and the local MP at the time was also contacted.

The community was also outraged regarding the lack of notification. The letter gave three weeks to object over the Christmas period. Local individuals living in The Square were interviewed: Nick Fletcher (from number 43), commented, 'It is clear they hoped to minimise response by the timing of the application'; Simon Kemp of Hyde End Road said, 'The health risks associated with high-power microwave radiation were of prime concern to people in the area, particularly its effects on babies and children; and since there was a child-minding business run in The Square the mast might ruin it!' In the end, the mast was not erected, and the community won the day!

People against masts, 2000

Chalfont Mead

As you approach the far corner of the 'parallelogram', you come across a driveway on your right: this property was built by William Wheeler and originally named 'Casseldene', but in 1965 it was renamed **Chalfont Mead** and numbered 14. The naming of Casseldene has been problematic for our research as it has been also spelt on documents as 'Cussell-dene', and assigned to different houses in the road. By 1892 a pair of semi-detached houses had been built by William on the bottom left hand corner of New Road (the section of The Square running from Basingstoke Road), both called 'Cussell-dene'. Later a house was built opposite also called 'Cussell-dene'. There was a connection found to this use of 'Cussell' as it was the maiden name of William's second wife Elizabeth, and also the middle name of his youngest son Harry. Harry, aged 22, is recorded on the St Michael's War Memorial as having died of his wounds on 29 August 1918.

Numbers 18 and 16, The Square (Jesmond is number 16, on the right)

**B** Continuing around the blind corner you come to the first of the more modern pairs of semi-detached houses, number 16, which is called **Jesmond**, and **number 18**, which – unusually for The Square – is unnamed. Daniel Mulhern bought the house now known as Chalfont Mead and resold it, retaining the orchard area, where this pair of houses was built in 1967. Number 16 initially sold for £4,970 and, according to a conveyance dated 14 June 1968, number 18 was sold to Mrs Nellie Coombs of Shinfield Green for £5,050.

Aerial View of Roselea/ Fairhaven and Wilcot

The next pair of semi-detached properties are again two of the original houses built in 1892 by Edwin Wheeler on land purchased from his brother William: **Fairhaven**, formerly known as 'Roselea', and **Wilcot** (numbers 20 and 22). The extension of Fairhaven was built using bricks from Caversham Bridge Hotel when it was destroyed by fire in the late 1980s. Wilcot was where the Wigmores started their cheese business. The *Village Maid Dairy* was established in 1986 in the garden shed of Wilcot by Anne and Andy Wigmore and now produces nationally renowned cheeses. Their original cheese was made from sheep's milk and was named 'Spenwood', after Spencers Wood. In May 1991 it won a prize at the International Food Exhibition at Earls Court. Anne, a former

Anne Wigmore, making cheese at Wilcot

cheesemaker at the National Institute for Research into Dairying, in Shinfield, said the business would always be a cottage industry. They were so successful in their production, they had to find larger premises and moved out of The Square to Hyde End Road in November 1987, and then later in November 1991 to Riseley. Village Maid Cheese also produces a soft Guernsey cheese called 'Waterloo'. The *Reading Chronicle* reported on 12 June 1998 that 'Wigmore' cheese was served at the dinner table on the Royal Yacht Britannia and was probably one of Riseley's best-kept secrets. Since then Anne and Andy have gone on to win many awards at the British Cheese Awards and World Cheese Awards with all three cheeses. If you're interested in reading more, have a look at their website, villagemaidcheese.co.uk.

Next door is another pair of the original semi-detached properties built by Edwin Wheeler in 1892, called **St Hilda** (number 24) and **Dilwyn** (number 26). Look up and note the characteristic white brick edging around the windows showing that they are two of the original houses. A family named Keil owned all four houses (numbers 20, 22, 24, and 26) for a period of time. Rosemary Holloway (née Edwards) lived in St Hilda from 1925 to 1963, and went to Lambs Lane School. The current owners moved into St Hilda in 1969: we know from them that this was the year that the ditches were removed from The Square, because they report that on viewing the property the ditches were there, but when they came to move in, the ditches were gone! These owners have built a number of extensions over the years: a kitchen in 1971, a side extension in 1979 and one into the loft in 1993, and their coalhole has been converted into a bathroom! They were kind enough to donate the photographs above. Dilwyn has changed its name twice over the years. Originally called 'Summeda', then 'Sunnyside', from 1925 it became 'Dilwyn', because the owner wanted to use the name of a house he had owned in Swallowfield.

St Hilda: in 1975 (*above left*); when an extension was being built in 1979 (*above right*); and in 2016 (*right*)

Dilwyn

Finally, nearing the end of the road, you approach two brand new semi-detached properties, completed in 2015 and as yet unnamed. They were built by the owner of number 26 on a plot where there was – until it was demolished in 2013 – a bungalow called **Tall Trees**. This bungalow was built in 1960 in the garden of Adey's Bakery – which we will come to in a moment – by descendants of the Adeys, for their daughter, Beryl Ballauff. Now it has been replaced by the two new houses.

Tall Trees, before it was demolished in 2013 (*above*), 28 and 30, The Square, now built on its site (*left*)

99

Now you will come to some double doors, which are sometimes open, but if the doors are shut the property is barely visible unless you look up and over the hedge. This is number **300, Hyde End Road**. Its rear entrance sits on The Square, but as you walk around the corner you can see the front of the house. This was another house built in the grounds of Adey's Bakery for one of their descendants. It has recently been sold to new owners.

Sheraton House and 300 Hyde End Road

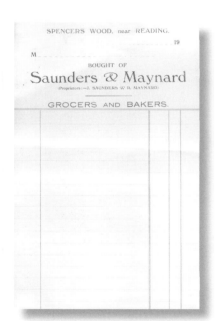

You are now at the Hyde End Road end of The Square. Turn the corner and start walking up Hyde End Road, back towards Whiteknights estate agents. Here is a property called **Sheraton House**, 300a Hyde End Road. It was originally a small business that has taken a variety of forms over the years. It was owned by a butcher, Thomas Ballard Pither, then it was a grocery and bakery called *Saunders & Maynard*. The 1911 census records from Saunders & Maynard are shown in the table below and their order pad is on the left. Around 1919 Harry Dukes Adey came from Wolverhampton, to become the master baker at Saunders & Maynard. He and his wife Sarah had a daughter, Elsie, who married Leonard Griffiths, also a baker. The family ran *Adey's Bakery* on this site until about 1963. Vic Earley recalled being sent by his mother to Adey's, and describes Miss Adey as being an 'absolute virtuoso at precise

### Extract from 1911 census for Saunders & Maynard

| Name | Relationship | Age | Status | Occupation | Birthplace |
|------|--------------|-----|--------|------------|------------|
| Martin James Saunders | Head | 33 | Married | Grocer | Aston Rowant, Oxon |
| Annie Saunders | Wife | 33 | Married | | Henley on Thames, Oxon |
| Reginald John Maynard | Partner | 26 | Single | Baker | Heckfield, Hants |
| Kate Everett | Sister-in-law | 25 | Single | Assisting in the business | Henley on Thames, Oxon |

guessing and never having to weigh anything'. In 1971 the bakery was sold to John Patrick O'Rourke, and thereafter called *Grovelands Store*, being run and managed by Iris O'Rourke. The business then became a private house, although the bakehouse in the garden still exists today and has been used as a studio by a local artist.

Adey's Bakery

Continue up Hyde End Road past Sheraton House, you will find two older semi-detached houses: number 302, Hyde End Road, is called **Rosedale**, and number 304 is **Newton Villa**. Recently a business called *Paradise Hair and Beauty* has been operating from Newton Villa, and you can often see the board on the pavement outside.

Penshurst Cottages, Rosedale and Newton Villa, early 1900s (*above*); Rosedale and Newton Villa 2016 (*left*)

**101**

Uphamhall
and Penshurst
Cottages

A pair of cottages, **2 and 1, Penshurst Cottages**, and a modern house called **Uphamhall**, built in 1993, bring you up to rear of Whiteknights and Miah's, and almost to the top of Hyde End Road.

**D** You have now come all the way around the 'parallelogram', but we haven't described the houses on the *other* side of The Square, so now you must double back on yourself and turn back into The Square, then cross over to the far side of the road.

Looking down
the Square
from Hyde End
Road, before
1969 when the
ditches were
filled in

**C** As you do, take a look down the road: the picture below shows how it looked before 1969 when the ditches were filled in. We will now look at the houses on the 'outside' of The Square.

Before you get to the first houses on the other side, you will pass a large garage, used by *Hyde End Studios*, which is run by professional photographer Simon Kemp. Spencers Wood Local History Group are extremely grateful to Simon for having created their Web site (swlhg.co.uk) and of course he has his own Web site, simonkempweddings.co.uk. Simon's studio was originally a pair of garages. Next you will come to another pair of semis, originally built by Edwin Wheeler – **1 and 2, Stanley Villas**, also known as numbers 43 and 41, The Square. They were sold in November 1890 to Mrs Elizabeth Wickens for £2,000. Both have been extended. Next door is another pair of semi-detached

1, Stanley Villas

**103**

Hope Cottage and Laburnum

houses – again built by Edwin Wheeler – called **Hope Cottage** and **Laburnum**. William Hinton lived at Hope Cottage and, during the years 1912–26 he was a churchwarden and sidesman at St Michael and All Angels Church. Hope Cottage was one of the properties which had gas and mains water by 1934.

The name of the second property has been spelt differently over the years: it has also been 'Laburnham Cottage'. Vic Earley spent his childhood living there and was kind enough to share his memories with us. Vic spoke of The Square being more appropriately termed 'The Parallelogram' because of its shape. His father rented Laburnum Cottage through most of Vic's formative years and he knew every 'gate, hedge, fence, ditch, almost every blade of grass.' It's apparent that, during the time he lived there, as with other properties in the road, there was no internal access to the toilet. A gas cooker was installed in 1942–43 and there was gas lighting throughout the house in the mid-1950s, when electricity was first supplied to the house. The family acquired a washing machine in 1962.

The Bird family from Laburnum enjoying The Square's street party in April 2011, celebrating the wedding of Prince William to Kate Middleton

Next door to Laburnum is another original property, **Hawthorne**. The white bricks around all the windows are visual evidence of its origins in the 1890s; the porch was added later. The house was built as a two-up, two-down worker's cottage, as many in The Square originally were. This one dates from 1895, and was bought by Alan and Jeannie Brice in 1998.

The land was originally owned by Edwin Wheeler, who sold it on 16 January 1888 to Walter Cuthbert, who was recorded in the 1891 census as a bootmaker and employer, aged 48. Wheeler then built 'Hawthorne Cottage' for him, completing it in 1895. An indenture (or land ownership document) shows that the house and land were sold in 1905 to William Hinton, a farmer. Mr Hinton then moved to Hope Cottage (next-door-but-one), selling to William Thomas Palmer in 1919. Mr Palmer was a retired house decorator and when he died the house passed to his son, William Thomas Palmer the younger. In 1935, Mrs Beatrice Mary Emblen bought Hawthorne Cottage from him and when she died in 1942 she left the house to her son Flight Sergeant William Emblen. Kelly's Directory (1929 and 1931) confirms that Mr Emblen had been an Insurance Agent. Hawthorne was one of the original properties of The Square, as shown on the 1899 Ordnance Survey map, and whilst being owned by only four individuals, the census shows that it was rented out and could have operated as a market garden at some point in the early 1910s.

Aerial View of Hawthorne

Continuing along to the properties adjacent, you will see there is a gap in the numbering. There have been applications to build on this land over the years, but they have always been rejected because of the blind bend.

The next houses we come to are **Alverne** (number 29) and **New Home** (number 27), which were probably built by William Wheeler about 1887 and have always been owned as a pair by the same landlords. On the 1911 census, when William George Cocks, a bricklayer, lived there with his family, Alverne was called 'Windmill Cottage'. A Mrs Blackwell rented Alverne; she and her daughter, Rosie, came to Spencers Wood as evacuees during the Second World

Syringa and
Wisteria

War. Before renting this house, they lodged with the Earleys at Laburnum. Two
generations of the Bradfield family lived in New Home from when it was built
until the 1990s – around one hundred years!

**B** Going round the corner of The Square, you will find **Syringa** (originally
called 'Casseldene') and **Wisteria** – numbers 25 and 23 – the first
pair of semi-detached houses built about 1887 by William Wheeler.
He himself lived here, using the large garden of number 23 as his builder's yard.
An article appeared in the *Reading Standard* on 10 October 1910, reporting an
'outbreak of fire', which started at the stable owned by William Wheeler and
'soon assumed alarming proportions, much to the terror of the neighbours, a
row of cottages in close proximity being endangered'. The newspaper reported
that Mr Jewell, with his son, Bertram, averted the danger, bringing:

> his own hose and reel and connect[ing them] to the newly erected
> standpipe. There were plenty of willing helpers and with their assistance
> especially that of Mr Downham and Mr Double's men, the fire was
> extinguished after two hours' hard work. The stable building was
> destroyed.

By 1949 the houses had acquired their present names, and until 1955 they
were owned by the same person but were then sold separately. In 1968 a corner
of the garden of Syringa was sold by Mr and Mrs B. Keenor to the Southern
Electricity Board for a substation, and you can regularly see cats sunbathing
on it on a warm day. On the other side of Wisteria is **number 21**, which does

Aerial View of
Rose Cottages

not have a name. This was originally the garden of Wisteria, and in 1970 the then occupant, Gilbert House, sold a parcel of land to builder A. J. Luckett who built the house.

Moving along to the row of cottages on your right, numbers 19, 17, 15, 11, The Square, or **numbers 4, 3, 2 and 1, Rose Cottages**. These we think are of a similar age to Syringa and Wisteria, built by William Wheeler, who sold the land and the row of cottages to his brother Edwin in 1892 for £70. Joseph Gale, grandfather of Marion Pyke, whom we met earlier, lived at Number 4, Rose Cottages before moving to Westview. Ken Wells lived at Number 1, Rose Cottages with his family. He used to be friends with Francis Benham of Ash and Harry Emblen of Hawthorne in the late 1940s and '50s. He went on to be a local policeman in Sonning and Wokingham, and then moved to the Metropolitan Police in 1962.

Many of the early properties were built with bricks from the Swain family kiln, at their brickyard on the 'Common'. White decorative bricks were fashionable then, and if you look at the white brick edging around the windows, you can tell which were the first houses built. On one of the original houses, Alfred Swain signed a brick.

9, The Square in 2016 (*right*) and when it was 'The Bungalow' in 1973 (*below*)

Next is **number 9**, The Square. In 1936 a piece of land was bought by a Mr Davis, who had a caravan sited there. In 1940 Shinfield Parish Council recorded 'that the attention of the Sanitary Officer be drawn to the fact that a party of about fifteen people are living under insanitary conditions on a plot of land situate in The Square Spencers Wood, owned by Mr N. Davis'.[7] Later a two-room bungalow was built, which was converted and extended several times over the years. In 1971 the converted bungalow was purchased and remodelled into a two-storey house, and most recently in 2013, has had a front extension added.

We then come up to a row of houses **numbers 7, 5a, 5, 3** and **1**, which were built in 1997 on the site of a property called **Oak Lodge**, a detached house

Oak Lodge (demolished in 1997)

full of character that had been lived in at one time by the Bailiff of Stanbury Estate, Edward Barrow, and later by Mr and Mrs Michael Barber. It was part of the Stanbury Estate sale in 1919, when it was listed as the 'picturesque small residence known as Oak Lodge', currently let to Mrs Smith Batten for £25 p.a.[8]

**End** Now you have come to the end of the walk. We hope we have shown you how The Square has evolved over the last 130 years. It is interesting to note that many of the original house names referred to trees and shrubs, such as Ash, Laburnum, Hawthorne, Oak and Wisteria, all lovely names that evoke the rustic origins of Spencers Wood.

Infill building since the 1990s has almost filled up The Square. Now the final two properties have been completed at number 28 and 30 ... do you think there is room for any more?

Looking back down The Square from Basingstoke Road (compare with the photo on p. 92)

## Notes

[1] For this chapter the authors consulted the censuses for 1871, 1881, 1891, 1901 and 1911; Ordnance Survey County Series, 1:2500, Berkshire (1872; 1st rev., 1899; 2nd rev., 1911; 3rd rev., 1937); Ordnance Survey National Grid, 1:2500, Title SU7166 (1968, 1983); school registers for Lambs Lane and Ryeish Green schools in the BRO; trade directories; electoral rolls and local newspapers. All the other information comes from the memories and records of current and past residents.

[2] *Our Village of Spencers Wood* (Spencers Wood Local History Group, 2001).

[3] 'Recollections', by Jack Povey. See Chapter Five. Jack lived in Spencers Wood for four years around 1893 and left when he was 11.

[4] 'Reminiscences', by Mrs E. Lowe. See Chapter Five.

[5] BRO D/N 44/1/1/1, Church Minutes..., 23 Nov. 1909: 'Reference was made to the gift of a New Organ for the Church, which has been presented by Mr Edwin Wheeler, in memory of his wife Anne Wheeler, who was one of the first members of this church, and who had taken an active part for many years in its work. The Secretary was asked to write to Mr Wheeler, expressing the thanks of the Church for the generous gift, and appreciation of the association [for] the same.'

[6] While researching for information about the Wheeler family, Jackie found this will at the BRO (EBb/B2/792/1). On reading the list, Jackie realised that details about Edwin and William's sister were sounding familiar. Fanny had married the brother, Joshua Bailey, of Jackie's second times great grandmother, Matilda Hamlin, née Bailey.

[7] BRO CPC 110/1/5, Shinfield Parish Council Minutes, 1937–1951, p. 94 31 Oct. 1940.

[8] Reading Local Studies Library, Nicholas of Reading, 1919, 'Stanbury Estate Sales Particulars'.

## CHAPTER NINE

# The Library

*Margaret Bampton*

S pencers Wood Branch Library is a Grade II listed building dating from 1890. It is situated on Basingstoke Road, opposite the junction with Hyde End Road. In the past century and a quarter, this pretty brick building has served as a school, cookery centre and library, and is a landmark of the village.[1]

### Spencers Wood School, 1890 to 1915

The need to educate all children was recognised in the mid-1800s when Britain was lagging behind the continent economically and the public demanded state education as in other European countries. This led to the 1870 Education Act, which established School Boards, and the 1880 Act, which compelled all children between the ages of 5 and 13 to attend school. Before these Acts, many poor children were educated in Church schools. Many of the Spencers Wood children would have gone to the Charles Russell School in Swallowfield or the

This chapter was produced with the help of Catherine Glover, who found additional material at the Berkshire Record Office.

Spencers Wood Infants' School, early 1890s

1481. Spencers Wood Schools.

Spencers Wood
Infants' School

Piggott School in Shinfield, until Frederick Allfrey of Stanbury provided the means to establish a school in Spencers Wood, on land he purchased from Miss Crowdy of Highlands. According to Pevsner, the school was designed by Smith & Son of Reading, and is 'pretty, with walls of grey vitrified brick and inventive red brick patterning as in a Persian rug'.[2] Allfrey officially opened the school

A tracing of the plan of Spencers Wood Infants' School, 1905 (BRO C/AR/ P4/102/2)

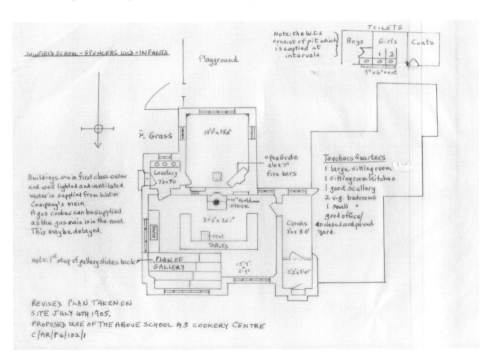

Children at Spencers Wood Infants' School, c.1905, with the names of some of the children written on the back: 'Medals: Gladys Cox, Elsie Lewendon, Willie Dearlove, Fred Dearlove, Sidney Randall, George Jones, Charles Jones; Prizes: Maud Davis, Daisy Swain, Dorothy Bissell, Bertha Frape, Percy Middleton, George Lappage, Fred Wyeth, Susan Clements, Elsie Lappage, Elizabeth Gearing, Elsie Bradfield, Dorothy Aldridge, Lily Clements, Winnie Foster, Ivy Bradfield, Edith Laplin'

on 15 September 1890, and his initials appear above the main door on the left, with the date to the right. On the left of the door is a benchmark showing the height above sea level: 66 metres.

Frederick Allfrey's initials and the date above the door of the School

The Headmistresses were:

Miss Scarratt
September 1890 to September 1899

Miss Walker
September 1899 to October 1900

Miss Growns
October 1900 to December 1901

Miss Wright
January 1902 to August 1915

Catherine Scarratt, the first Headmistress, was required by law to provide a progress report every week in the Log Book, and what follows are extracts from this book.[3] At first the reports were extensive but the enthusiasm wore off as the years went by. The curriculum consisted of arithmetic, reading, writing, knitting, needlework (which was taught to the boys, who seemed rather afraid of it, for the first time in February 1891), singing, drill and object lessons. Object lessons were listed each year in the Log Book and for the year of 1892, they were:

Animals: cow, horse, sheep, goat, elephant, lion, tiger, camel, whale, cat etc.
Birds: cuckoo, swallow, robin.
Minerals: gold, silver, iron, coal, chalk.
Trades: blacksmith, carpenter, baker, shoemaker, tailor.
Form and Colour: six of each. The last items were eventually considered too elementary.

The Headmistress reported that the children were using their new cubes and tablet laying.

The Log Book records school closures. The first closure was to put up curtains at the large windows. In the very first term, the school closed for three weeks because of an outbreak of measles, as it was often to do again. In January and April 1892, there were outbreaks of whooping cough, and in other years, diphtheria and scarlet fever. On many occasions the school was closed because of bad weather. In December 1890, the school closed for ten days because of deep snow and in March 1891 only two children arrived when again there was deep snow. Sometimes wet, stormy weather caused the roads and the playground to be flooded. On one occasion the children could not go outside and had to walk around the classroom for their break. On another, some of the boys were blown into a ditch and nearly drowned on their way home from school.

The school had the capacity for 97 children and the numbers on the register varied from 47 in the first year to 69 in 1904. There was a Kindergarten, Standard I and Class II. Children from Standard I often went on to other schools. Frederick Allfrey and Miss Henrietta Crowdy, who lived at Highlands, visited the school on many occasions, as did several ministers from local churches. They would listen to recitations such as *The Child and the Bird* and *The Cobweb*. They would listen to the children singing accompanied by an organ, examine the children's knitting and question them. The boys' needlework 'was going on nicely'. In 1894, Matilda Farmer had taken the first prize for her sewing at 'The Show', presumably the Swallowfield Show, and Violet Wheeler had taken the second prize the previous year.

Once a year, usually in the summer, there would be a Scripture Examination by one of the local ministers. The first report contained the following:

The discipline, order and tone are excellent and the general condition reflects credit on the teacher. Some of the children were shy in answering and their replies were not general enough but doubtless they will improve. It is recommended that they ought to know the first part of the Catechism, the Christian Covenant, in addition to the Creed, the Lord's Prayer and the Ten Commandments. But on the whole the condition of the school is very satisfactory. It is doing a very useful work and will prove itself a great benefit to the neighbourhood.

The following year, 1892, the report was similar except that the defective answers were blamed on the very hot weather and that the children should be taught some simple explanations of the Baptismal Covenant. Many children were commended, see the list on the right, and after the exam in 1897, the year of Queen Victoria's Golden Jubilee, those that were commended were given a Jubilee sixpence. Many of these children attended the Congregational chapel in Chapel Lane, almost opposite the school.

The school year started in January and consisted of four quarters: the first quarter went to Easter, the second to Whitsuntide, the third to the Harvest Holidays (four weeks in August), and the fourth to the end of November. In December, Her Majesty's Inspector would visit the school and file his report in the following January. Much depended on this report as it determined whether the school would receive an adequate Aid Grant in the following year. In the last quarter of 1891 the grant was withheld and the children had to pay fees for that quarter. Many years passed before these fees were refunded. The school report that appeared in February 1892, praised the first year of the school by saying:

### Scripture Examination commendations

**1892**
Lowe, Webb, Swain, Bowyer, Crockford, Double, Wheeler, Bennett, Cordery, Norris, Povey*, Farmer.

**1894**
Maud Mitchell, Matilda Farmer, William King, George Cox, Ethel Lewendon, Edward Cox.

**1895**
Henry Cordery, Albert Benham, Mabel Swain, Ethel Lewendon, Alice Bowyer, Matthew Farmer, Violet Wheeler.

**1896**
James Double, George West, Laurence White, John Povey*, Kate Miles.

**1897**
Winifred Smith, Lucy Benham, Edith Bennett, Lilian Gibson. These all received a Jubilee sixpence.

**1898**
Reginald Smith, Wilfred Hopkins, Harold White, Edith Bennett, Kate Miles.

**1899**
Alice Bradfield, Daisy Crockford, Helen Reeves, Charles Norris, Sophia Swain, Dora Wheeler, Percival Double, Walter Luckwell.

* John Povey was known as Jack. His memories about the Chapel appear in Chapter Five.

This handsome, well built school, has commenced its useful career with very fair promise. With the exception of the arithmetic of the first standard, the elementary attainments are pretty good. Drill, singing and Kindergarten exercises are fair and the needlework is good.

So the boys did well! In other years, the reports are similar, about arithmetic in particular, but they grow less detailed as the years pass. One year the Inspector complained that the doors opened inwards and that the cloakroom pegs were insufficient and that nothing had been done about either. Another year the report criticised the musical drill for its lack of vigour and the Inspector was unable to recommend the grant for singing by note. The annual report in 1896 said that too much attention was given to some individuals and that the inattention of the rest of the class often escaped observation!

Attendance varied from time to time according to the weather and sickness. One year the attendance on the first day of one quarter was very good because the next day there was a half holiday treat by Mr and Mrs Allfrey. Once, the attendance was very thin, because of drenching rain with the playground half under water. Another time the children were away with swollen faces. In 1892, another treat was given by Miss Crowdy, who made the children go into the playground at 3.30 p.m. for a run; on returning to their desks they were presented with heaps of cake and bread and butter, which soon disappeared. When this was over, they had a scramble for sweets and, afterwards, a pair of warm cuffs knitted in the school, and a pretty Christmas card was given to everyone. They all thanked Miss Crowdy for her kindness. Then, after singing a hymn, each child was given an orange and all went home delighted with their treat. The previous year, at Christmas, the children had been presented with picture books, prayer books or a pretty picture, but no tea. At the end of the 1892 school year, some six boys and six girls were presented with shoes, two pairs of stockings and capes.

There was another tea in February 1893, given by Mr Allfrey and arranged by Miss Crowdy, at which the children entertained their mothers and were spoken to by the Rev. St Aubyn about the Post Office Savings Bank. By March the same year, the children had between them saved 13/3d. This was banked by Miss Crowdy. In 1894, a bell, purchased by Mr Allfrey, was introduced to bring the children in and every child wanted to ring it. At Christmas that year, the girls received frocks, warm cloaks, petticoats and pinafores, whereas the boys received shoes, two pairs of stockings (six of which had been knitted in school) and all received knitted cuffs. The babies had toys, dolls and picture books. The following year, the presents were restricted to those who had been the most regular in attendance. The most regular of the girls received work boxes and dolls, and the boys were given warm stockings whilst others had picture books. In 1896, the children received petticoats, six of which were knitted in school, pieces of stuff (woollen material) for frocks, and nightgowns for the girls, and pieces of shirting, stockings or two pocket handkerchiefs for the boys. This year they all took home a slice of cake and a handful of sweets.

The school was closed once when there was a Church Choir excursion and again, when there was a Sunday School treat. In September 1896, the Medical Officer decided not to close the school because of measles and poor attendance, but in November it closed for three weeks for that very reason. In the year 1897 (Queen Victoria's Jubilee), the school closed for the Shinfield Festival; the next day only 28 children attended and 'they looked very sleepy and were sent home to have a good rest'. That year there was a festival at Swallowfield and a Band of Hope Fete, which most of the children went to, again missing school. There was also the Grazeley Choir trip to Oxford, when the school closed again. That particular year the present at Christmas was a useful piece of warm clothing, but because she had been absent for only one half day, Lucy Benham was given a workbox well filled with cottons, needles and pins, and so on. The report said that Her Majesty's Inspector thought it not unreasonable to expect a larger number of subscriptions – by private individuals – to the school. HMI also made a grant of £10 for the increase in salaries and wished the school would do more in raising subscriptions.

In the next year, a new monitress-teacher, called Mazella Horner, started but, unfortunately, she immediately contracted influenza and the lessons were taken by the assistant Miss Hawkins. The Christmas party saw the children singing some of their songs, having a flag drill, playing a game called the Railway Train and sitting down to tea. All this was by courtesy of Miss Crowdy, who presented them with an article of warm clothing. The school report said that:

> all was in good order except the babies who appeared to be beyond the control of the young monitress to whose sole care they were left. There was an absence of the life and brightness that characterises a good infant school.

This report was received in March 1899 and the Headmistress resigned in July. A new Headmistress, Miss Walker, started in September and found that Standard I was not up to the level of efficiency expected. Rug making was introduced and object lessons omitted but French knitting, embroidery and boxes of letters substituted instead. Drill became musical drill and the children were given a half-day holiday for an evening lecture. The grant at the end of 1900 amounted to £20. The £10 given earlier was for equipment repairs, improvement of the premises, furniture, apparatus, books, stationery, better instruction of pupil teachers and maintaining salaries. The school was to be inspected to ensure this was carried out. In 1900, the babies received four new desks and the Harvest Holidays were extended to six weeks. Miss Walker resigned after one year and Miss Growns took over. She found that discipline was poor and the children all talking, so there needed to be changes made.

During 1901, several children left the school, to be taught at a little school held in Miss Scarratt's house. Was this the former Headmistress? The children's names were retained, nevertheless, on the school register. The annual report said that 36 new slates had arrived, the worst subject was arithmetic as the children guessed the answers, and the gallery should be fitted with desks. Violet Wheeler, a former pupil, was a monitress and she had been praised many times for her ability. When she left the school the Log Book recorded that it was a pity that it wasn't the other assistant who had left (despite the rule about not recording personal opinions in the Log Book). Miss Growns was the only Headmistress who recorded any punishments. Was it this or the personal comments that led to her leaving in December? There is no record of her resignation: there is a record of her having an appointment before December but, by the following January, Mrs Wright was the Headmistress.

Only 33 attended on Mrs Wright's first day, the day Frederick Double was admitted. Leonard Swain returned to school after an absence of six weeks due to scarlet fever. As this disease was also present in the school house next door, the children were obliged to play in the southern half of the playground only. The school year now ended in March and not November. In April 1902, the school was scrubbed and cleaned. In later years the monitress was made to sweep and dust the school, keeping the children waiting in the playground. When the Prince and Princess of Wales visited Reading, the children had tea on the lawn of Stanbury and, in June, the school closed for a week on account of the Coronation of Edward VII. (There was also a week off in 1911, for the coronation of King George V.) By September, the numbers had increased to 51 and the children had readers and writing books and used lead pencils. The slates had gone and by 1904 they were using pens and ink. The children often went for walks in the grounds of Highlands or Stanbury looking for berries, seed pods, bluebells, and so on, according to the season. Some years, weather permitting, lessons were held out of doors. At the end of 1902, the children entertained their mothers with songs, drills and recitations. This was followed in the early part of the next year by a concert.

In 1903, there was a Band of Hope outing and in June the playground was flooded. In the same month, however, the children had a tea in the schoolroom with games and races afterwards. The distribution of prizes was made at Highlands. Silver medals were given to those who had perfect attendance. Several people acted for the Headmistress while she was absent for three months and the writing in the Log Book changed. The classes were rearranged: the Baby Class was in the classroom taken by a monitress, the First and Second Infants were taken in the larger room by the Assistant Mistress and Standards I and II were at the gallery end, taken by the Headmistress. An epidemic of measles caused the school to be closed for eight weeks and the summer holidays were reduced to three weeks as a result. Some children left to go to the Swallowfield and Shinfield schools. As Lambs Lane School was due to be opened in 1908, a notice was received to say that after 1906, no child under five was to be admitted. For the first time a tree was decorated at Christmas and this year the children received a toy or doll as a present, and the boys were given useful garments while the girls received material for dresses.

By 1904, the numbers had risen to 69 children, 17 of them under five years of age. The school had received ten new desks that year and in 1910 ten dual desks were removed.

During 1906, the school treat was at Grazeley. The HMI report required that the creepers be cut back from the windows of the main room and the panes cleaned. The Inspector also said that a ball frame on a stand, a thermometer for each room, some more pictures, and a 'mariner's compass' was required in the school. He also recommended that the gallery be removed, which upset Mr Allfrey, who wrote to the Board of Education saying that the school was his freehold property and he felt it most unfair for the Board to ask him to remove the gallery when he had done everything to please them in 1890 in building it. When the new school was built in Lambs Lane, the numbers would drop at Spencers Wood so the gallery would not be in the way. But if the Board insisted on removing the gallery, they could do so providing they made good the walls, floors and so on, removing the iron rails on which part of the gallery runs back.

The following year, water was laid on in the lavatories and the Inspector requested roller towels to be installed. The gallery was still in place! When Lambs Lane School opened in 1908, 20 children left the school, which meant that 43 were left on the books and Standard I was removed. In the same year, when the new church of St Michael and All Angels was dedicated, the children were given a half-day holiday. The Diocesan report said that it was a capital little school and HMI said that the children were bright and happy, controlled with much kindness and tact, and taught with intelligence, skill and success. In 1910, thirteen children went to other schools, some to Ryeish Green, which had just opened.

By 1911, there were only 34 children on the books; eight more left for other schools in March. That year's report said that the children's knowledge of numbers, reading and handwriting was good. Voice training was now given in singing lessons. It was recorded in 1912 that the children were taken for a slide on the pond after having a few lessons called 'On Ice'. There were celebrations on Empire Day and in June, a fire was lit to dry out the children's clothes and boots because they were very wet. By 1913, there were only 25 enrolled and this continued until 1915, when the school closed. Frederick Card, aged five, was admitted in 1914 as Lambs Lane was too far for him to walk. Vera Halfacre was admitted in the last year. In June of 1915, the school closed for an epidemic of whooping cough and reopened with only 15 on the books. On 23 July, there was a very poor attendance and the Stock and Stores Clerk attended to list the stock. Finally on 29 July 1915, the last entry reads: 'With deep regret, I this day resign charge of the school', signed by 'E Wright'.

In April 1914, Frederick Allfrey wrote to the County Council that he was 'willing to leave the School as proposed for purely educational purposes, not as a sick house, etc'. In May the Council agreed to lease the school as a Cookery and Manual Instruction Centre, but then Allfrey and the other School Managers (Miss Crowdy of Highlands and Mr and Mrs Charles Millett) had thought better of the idea and withdrew the offer. When Mr Allfrey died the following year the school closed. In 1918, Capt. Moubray Allfrey of Greenways, Chippenham, and Frederick Vere Allfrey of Ashridgewood, Wokingham, leased the building to the Local Education Authority and it reopened as a further education centre, where carpentry was taught in the small room at the back and cookery in the large room at the front. Allfrey's estate, including the library and school house, was auctioned in May 1919, much of it being purchased by Charles Allen, and in 1920 Mr Allen sold the land and building to Berkshire County Council.[4] Billy Wilson could remember learning carpentry there and it became his trade: he built his own house at Lane End, Beech Hill Road in the 1930s. Evening classes were held here from 1931 and children from Three Mile Cross school attended. Their memories can be found in our book about Ryeish Green School. The carpentry was stopped during the Second World War because of the shortage of wood and the kitchen was placed in the back room instead whilst the large room was used for tables and school dinners.

When in 1920 Berkshire County Council purchased the Cookery Centre, for £1,500, they were bound by a covenant made between Henrietta Crowdy and Frederick Allfrey, to maintain a wrought-iron fence or an oak cleft pole fence between the school site and Highlands on the south and west sides.[5] It looks as if the fence there today might be the original one. Another covenant stated that no building on that land should be used for the sale of wine, beer or spirituous liquors of any kind whatsoever.

### Cookery Centre, 1941 to 1947

There is a Log Book for this period, starting in May 1941 when the former school, at the time a Domestic Science Centre, was designated as a wartime communal feeding centre.[6] All villages had to have a feeding centre in case of emergencies and the building held blankets and supplies for this. The centre may never have been used for emergencies, but it was used for both making and serving hot dinners for Lambs Lane School. The older girls from Lambs Lane helped Mrs Greening, the cook, to prepare the meal for 26 diners on the first occasion, when Mr Dawson and Miss Vowles attended. Dorothy Cripps can remember Miss Vowles teaching her when she came from Beech Hill School for lessons. Four of them would arrive in Doug Double's taxi to help the cook prepare the meals to take back to Beech Hill. Once on returning to Beech Hill the taxi went over a bridge too rapidly and Joyce Wells' soup went everywhere in the taxi but Dorothy's rice pudding stayed put as it was rather stiff!

Rosemary Holloway said that her mother, Mrs Edwards, helped out Mrs Bond as her assistant. Mrs Bond followed Mrs Greening. Then there was Miss Woodward, who taught all the other schools that attended there from Riseley, Farley Hill, Shinfield, Grazeley, Beech Hill and Ryeish Green. The lessons were very basic and consisted of making oatmeal biscuits, sausage rolls, scones, Cornish pasties and chocolate cake, and after the first summer they learned yeast cookery. They also learned about first aid and unrationed meats like mince, sausage meat, and liver. These were made into patties, pies and puddings. The younger girls learned to scrub the chairs, lay the tables and wait at them, arrange the flowers, and wash up the dishes.

Sometimes the centre closed when Miss Woodward went to help other feeding centres such as Woodley, Mortimer and Arborfield and to learn about fruit preservation. Her knowledge was then passed onto the children who made

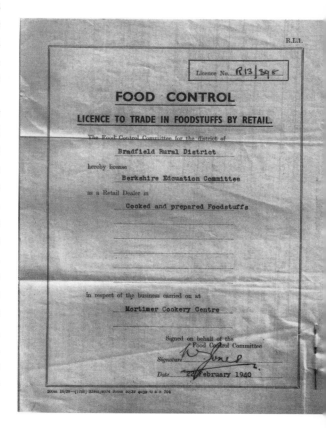

Food Licence, February 1940, for Mortimer Cookery Centre

jams from rhubarb and marrows, and bottled fruits such as apple and blackberries according to the season. There were other reasons for closure when the Army took over for a month in September 1941, and in October when the children helped with the potato harvest.

During the first three months of 1942, very little cookery was done as the teacher was ill and the writing in the Log Book changed frequently as if different people were in charge. In early April the centre closed completely for six weeks, and there was no cookery at all until September. In January 1943, the cookery continued and the girls looked after the canteen laundry. Twice classes were delayed because of a late dinner at Shinfield School and a bus strike. The community feeding appears to stop in the summer of 1943, and from September the lessons were of plain cookery, such as cakes and scones and no Christmas cake, but much housewifery and laundry. Perhaps this was because of food shortages. All the centres required a food licence: Spencers Wood was under the supervision of the Mortimer centre and therefore covered by its food licence.

From 1944, reporting in the Log Book changed, each school now being shown separately, and from September 1945 cookery instruction began in earnest. The girls now learned about soups and stews; cakes; sultana, meat and cheese puddings; ginger and cheese biscuits; sausage and egg pie; vegetable pie; pancakes; yeast and baking powder breads; sausage rolls; jam buns or puffs; potato scones; semolina and macaroni puddings; Irish Stew; custard; Queen of Puddings; oatmeal sausages and soup; Scotch Broth; Toad-in-the-Hole; Rothesay Pudding; Patriotic Pudding; Brazilian Stew; and Emergency Bread. Rothesay Pudding is a steamed suet pudding containing jam, and Patriotic Pudding also contained jam and could be made with grated carrot, or grated potato, and grated lemon or orange rind ('if available').[7] But what were Brazilian Stew and Emergency Bread like?

Reg Norriss can remember using the centre for cookery classes with a dozen others, cooking on the range, and could remember eating nettles instead of cabbage for school dinners.

During 1945, when Grazeley School was used as a Polling Station the children did not attend the centre. The Log Book ends in 1946 as the curriculum was changing due to the 1944 Education Act, which brought in secondary schools. From 1947, all the schools that used the cookery centre became infant and junior schools with the exception of Three Mile Cross School at Ryeish Green, which became the local secondary school. The building then took on a different role in the community.

### The Library, 1947 Onwards

In 1924, Berkshire County Council (BCC) accepted a grant of £1,600 from the Carnegie Trust to set up stationary collections of library books, as per the Public Library Act 1923, in individual villages; these were to be managed by volunteers. Although Spencers Wood Library was not one of the 110 set up that first year, during the 1950s the building began to be used as a library.

After the War, the building was known as the Handicraft Centre and, according to Betty Robertson, Ryeish Green School (now established as a secondary school through the Education act of 1944) used it for cookery and woodwork classes. Betty came to Spencers Wood in 1957 to teach at Lambs Lane School – now a junior school – and lodged with the Warners at Balimore in Basingstoke Road until she moved to Reading in 1968; until 1990, however, she continued to teach at Lambs Lane. Betty remembered that, for a period of time, the local Mother and Baby Clinic used the premises before it was eventually moved to the Village Hall (see Chapter Eleven). Betty also said that there was a small library in the back room (presumably where the children's library is today), which was open once or twice a week lending well-worn fiction books. The Headmaster of Lambs Lane School, Reginald Taylor, lived in the house adjoining the library, with his wife and family. They had an attractive front garden with flower beds and shrubs, and at the back was an extensive vegetable garden with fruit bushes and trees. When the Taylors left in 1966, the new Headmaster, Ivan Webster, and his family moved in. Betty recalls that the house was rather gloomy inside, but they set to and, in one weekend, decorated the whole house in white.

In 1963, Christ the King Roman Catholic Church offered to purchase the building, then known as the 'Special Subjects Centre', for £15,000, so that they could build a small church on the site, for 110 worshippers. Obviously this did not come to pass, although the Church was holding services for an hour each Sunday morning in 1969. From 1967, Berkshire County Council Library Committee also paid rent for the building for one hour a week for library purposes. By 1969 the building was being referred to as 'the *former* Handicraft Centre', and the Roman Catholics were the only people making any use of it. Mr Webster, the tenant of The School House, offered to buy the house if the County Council was intending to sell it, but although he moved to a different school in Newbury later that year, he was still renting the house in 1971. In that year, 1971, the County Council decided to appropriate the house for 'Library Purposes', and the following year The School House was let to a member of the County Planning Office staff.[8] Later it was let to librarians from Berkshire County Council's Education Library Services. Patricia Green can remember that when she first came to live in Spencers Wood in the early 1970s the library was being run, not by BCC but by three volunteer ladies. Because they were unpaid they would not charge any fines on late returns. It was only later that BCC started running a library with paid librarians. The small room was heated by a stove before central heating was installed.

In 1974, BCC applied for planning permission to build a new library on the site of the Handicraft Centre to service the area south of Reading. This was refused on the grounds that the site was unsuitable because of the traffic hazard on the A33 (this was before the opening of the by-pass, so they were referring to Basingstoke Road, now the B3349). Another suggestion was that the Handicraft Centre should be sold and a property in Hyde End Road purchased instead, costing half as much and without the traffic problems.[9] This too, was abandoned because of capital cuts to the 1975/6 County Plan. In 1979 BCC were still thinking about what to do with the building, as the following paragraph appears in the Local District Plan:

> The library services in the area are provided by the Council by means
> of a mobile library service supplemented by a permanent library centre

in Basingstoke Road which is open for one and a half hours per week on a Monday evening. Current schedules for the mobile service provide for fortnightly visits to all parts of Spencers Wood and schedules have recently been revised to improve the services by concentrating more library time in those settlements where demand is greatest. A trailer may be introduced which could be stationed for longer periods in the area until a more permanent site is found.[10]

In 1980, Shire Hall was built in Shinfield Park and the County Libraries Service was operated from there. In 1983 Sheila Jones was the branch librarian at Spencers Wood and she was writing the Library column in *Spencers Wood and Three Mile Cross News*. There was a lot of interest in chess in the village and after a very successful Under-14 Chess Tournament they started a chess club in the Library on Monday evenings: adults as well as children came to the first meeting. Two years later it was still going strong but the organiser, Ivan Sayer, had gone to live in Cairo for two years. John Norris took over from him but couldn't always come on Mondays to help with the club, mainly attended by children aged 7–10. Sheila reminded people, in her column, that books could be renewed (once only!) over the telephone or by letter as well as in person. The Library acquired a microfiche reader in 1983, with *British Books In Print* and the BCC Library Catalogue available in that format. In 1985 the column reminded readers that the Library has 'many tourist and town guides, pointing out places of interest and listing accommodation available. Why not save yourself time and postage by spending an hour in the library checking out the brochures.' It also ran a special exhibition of Virago books, 'by some of the greatest living writers of our time that had been out of print for many years'. The Librarian announced that 'During the past few weeks I have collected a considerable amount of lost property. As well as the usual bookmarks and postcards, there are a few discarded gloves and hats and child's anorak. Someone has again left stamps in the Stanley Gibbons catalogue. ... the Library has many books about gardening ... sewing ... swimming ... [and] mountain climbing'. In 1986, a photocopier was installed and was proving useful for 'taking copies of reference material for homework etc'. It cost 10p a copy. The Librarian pointed out that Library fines had been increased in January 1986 and 'are proving very expensive indeed. For example a book previously charged at 25p is now charged at 75p'. In 1987, Kate Saunders was the main librarian at Spencers Wood and she took over the column. There was now a 'Village Diary' in the Library: 'All entries are welcome. Jumble Sales, Fetes, Meetings. Sports Fixtures etc. Be in the know.' She also wrote a column in the magazine called 'Book Look': in March of that year for example, she reviewed *Duffy is Dead* by J. M. O'Neill. The same year the WRVS were advertising in the magazine 'for two ladies to exchange library books every three weeks to the house bound', and in December there was 'SNOWFUN TIME at the Library – "a video, stories, crafts and games"'.[11]

Librarians worked closely with schools and organised book events and talks. In 1993/94, the library service provided books for elderly, disabled and house-bound people by visiting hospitals, residential homes such as Spring Gardens and day centres. The county bought 100,000 new books for 43 static libraries, 11 container libraries (one at Arborfield), and mobile libraries visited 322 communities including Spencers Wood.

It is not known when the title passed from BCC to Wokingham District Council, but it was Wokingham that sold The School House in 1993, granting easements regarding the utilities and space shared with the library. In 1994, a covenant was made that parts of the land were subject to leases for 325 years. When BCC was replaced by the new Wokingham District Unitary Authority in 1994, responsibility for the Library Service transferred to Wokingham.

Before the library system was computerised, the books contained small identity cards in a pocket (*right*). Borrowers were provided with different coloured cards for different categories borrowed such as fiction, non-fiction, music and so on. When the book was borrowed, its card was removed and placed inside the borrower's card (which also contained a pocket) and retained by the library, filed in a date due-back tray in author order. The book was stamped with the date due back as it is today. On the return of the books, the librarian had to feverishly look through all the borrowers' cards to replace the cards in the books and return the borrower's card to its owner. Libraries used to be very popular and queues would form, but when Linda Rex joined the service in 1996, the popularity of the library service was slowing down: to encourage more borrowers, events were planned. One of the most popular events was 'Storytime' for the children, presented by volunteer Margaret Stead, an ex-schoolteacher. Volunteers were encouraged and the library currently hosts two craft classes and two book clubs run in the afternoons and evenings. Another popular event for children was 'Zoo Lab.', where small animals (live ones!) were brought in for them to look at.

Library card, before computerisation

According to Linda, who was the librarian at Spencers Wood from 1996 to 2015, the Arborfield container library (which dates from before 1996) was recently vandalised and may be replaced by a 'pop-up library'. There is still demand for library services as the number of cassettes, videos, CDs and books

Spencers Wood
Library in 2016

borrowed during this period has increased, and when Arborfield Garrison is redeveloped there are plans for a new school and library there.

The library was closed for a short while in 2003 when automatic doors and a toilet with baby changing facilities were installed. At one time, Spencers Wood Local History Group held an exhibition there. Wokingham Borough's current plan is to use more volunteers or casual librarians to run the Library and events. Since the 1970s this lovely building has been our library and, despite cutbacks being made, we hope it will always remain so.

## Notes

[1] In addition to the sources cited, the following have been used in this chapter: Joan Dils, *100 years of Public Service. A history of Berkshire County Council* (1990), Spencers Wood Local History Group, *History of Ryeish Green School* (2010); memories of Dorothy Cripps, Barbara Debney, Patricia Green, Rosemary Holloway, Reg Norris, Linda Rex, Betty Robertson.

[2] BRO C/CL/E4/74/3, Berkshire County Council correspondence about Spencers Wood School, 1903–1973, Letter from BCC to J. E. Gibson, Solicitors of Trustees of the late Capt. Freville Cookson, owners of Highlands, 26 May 1925; G. Tyack, S. Bradley and N. Pevsner, *Berkshire* (The Buildings of England, 1966, 2nd edn, 2010), p. 528.

[3] BRO C/EL 20, Spencers Wood School Log Book, 1890–1914.

[4] BRO, C/CL/E4/74/1, BCC correspondence about Spencers Wood School Lease, 1914–1920, Letter from Allfrey to W. C. F. Anderson, 29 Apr. 1914; C/CL/E4/74/3, Memo from Allfrey to Berkshire Education Committee, 7 Sept. 1903; C/CL/E4/74/1, Extracts from the minutes of the Byelaws and School Attendance Sub-Committee, 9 May and 13 June 1914; C/CL/E4/74/1, Lease dated 6 June 1918; C/CL/E4/74/1, Letter from Nicholas (Fraser and Russell), 31 May 1920. When the County

Council was dissolved, the title passed to Wokingham District Council and then to Wokingham Borough Council.

[5] BRO C/CL/E4/74/2, BCC correspondence about Spencers Wood School, 1920–1926, Conveyance, 29 Sept. 1920.

[6] BRO, SCH 26/8/1 Spencers Wood Domestic Science Centre Log Book, 1941–1947.

[7] Secrets of Self-Sufficiency, secrets-of-self-sufficiency.com/rothesay-pudding, accessed 9 May 2016; Wartime Recipes, recipespastandpresent.org.uk/wartime/, accessed 9 May 2016.

[8] C/CL/E4/74/3, Memo from Rev. Patrick Collins, Christ the King, Northumberland Ave. to the County Valuer, 6 June 1963; C/CL/E4/74/3, Memo of Education Committee, 18 July 1969; C/CL/E4/74/3, Memo to County Treasurer, 20 Mar. 1967; C/CL/E4/74/3 Letter from Webster to Clerk to the County Council, 21 Oct. 1969; Memo, 3 Nov. 1969; County Valuer's Report, 16 July 1971; C/CL/E4/74/3, Memo, 3 Aug. 1971; Memo, 21 Sept. 1972.

[9] *Reading Chronicle*, 8 Nov. 1974.

[10] Wokingham District Council, *Spencers Wood District Plan* (1979).

[11] *Spencers Wood and Three Mile Cross News*, Jan. 1983, Feb. 1983, May 1983, Jan. 1985, Mar. 1985, Apr. 1985, Mar. 1986, May 1986, Mar. 1987, July 1987, Dec. 1987.

CHAPTER TEN

# The Church of St Michael and All Angels

*Catherine Glover*

T he church of St Michael and All Angels is the parish church of Spencers
Wood, situated at the north end of the village, on the eastern side of
Basingstoke Road next to the Village Hall. Its history takes us from an
era in which a growing population needed a new church with its own Vicar,
through two world wars to a period of social change that led to several parishes
being combined to create a larger unit, served by a team of clergy: the United
Benefice of Loddon Reach. As the church building is modern, there have not
been many changes to its fabric and those have been recent: they are described
at the end of the chapter.

### Too many parishioners, not enough churches

In 1907 there was no Anglican church in Spencers Wood. The population
had grown to over 500 and the Vicar of Grazeley had been 'kindly carrying
on the Sunday afternoon services, in the schoolroom'. The Vicars of Shinfield,
Swallowfield and Grazeley parishes, Messrs C. F. Millett and H. L. Hunter and
Dr Woodforde formed a committee: Hunter promised to donate the site for the
church, a stipend fund for a Curate was set up, and a building fund started with
promises of money from the Misses Crowdy and Forbes, Messrs Millett, Hunter,
Benyon, and Palmer, Capt. and the Hon. Mrs Allfrey, and the Rural Dean, the Rev.
C. Lovett Cameron. The building was designed by Spencer Slingsby Stallwood,
FSA, of Reading, and built by local builder Charles Aldridge, nephew of Edwin
Wheeler, whom we have met already in Chapters Five and Eight.[1]

The foundation stone was laid on the first day of 1908 by Mr Hunter and, in
March the same year, a decision was made to 'complete the Nave, including the
Chancel Arch' for the sum of £1,700, with the intention of building a temporary
wall at the far end of the nave until funds for a chancel could be obtained.
However, once the nave was completed, Hunter offered to complete the chancel
and vestry at his own expense. This resulted in a church 96 feet long, with a
nave 27 feet wide, south porch, chancel and vestry, seating for 270, and central

Architect's drawing of St Michael's (BRO D/P 194/28/6/2)

heating but – like the rest of the village – no electricity. The 'good' East window is by Powell and sons. The gardens were laid out by Mr David Prior and his son George, with yew trees to the north and a magnolia on the south-facing side near the vestry door. A garden fete and sale of work in July raised just over £100 for the Furnishing Fund. Dr Woodforde died before the church was finished and

St Michael's under construction in 1908

THE CHURCH SPENCERS WOOD

is commemorated on the font cover. The church of St Michael and All Angels, Spencers Wood, was dedicated on Michaelmas day, 1908.[2]

At the start, the Curate-in-Charge was the Rev. Frederick Temple Lewarne (b. 1870 in Lanivet, Cornwall) and the church was licensed for holy communion and baptisms, the first of which was held on 10 October 1908. It was no ordinary affair: Robert and Annie Middleton, whom we met in Chapter Eight, had no fewer than five of their children christened on this momentous occasion.[3]

In 1910 the church was closed for a week while a new organ was installed. According to the *Reading Mercury*, leading members of the congregation had started to seek ways of financing an organ soon after the church was opened: they received £100 from Andrew Carnegie, the American philanthropist (1835–1919), whose interest in music had led him to fund the building of about 7000 church organs, and they matched this with another £100. The newspaper article describes the organ as 'a fine instrument with two manuals and 14 stops ... designed and erected by Messrs. C. H. Walker and Sons, 25 Manchester-street, London and Reading ... a small organ of great powers, and possessing delicate sweetness of tone and expression'. The organ dedication was presided over by Mr Greville Palmer and in the afternoon 'the church was crowded with an audience that listened with delight to the exquisite rendering of [organ music]' in a recital by Mr A. C. P. Embling from St Laurence's Reading, with violin solos by Miss Bacon of Swallowfield.[4]

The church had a choir of 18 men and one boy, who wore surplices, and enjoyed outings to Caversham Bridge in Jim Earley's coal lorry. In 1909 there

Interior of St Michael's c.1908, before the installation of the organ on the south side of the chancel

Clergy entering St Michael's, possibly for the consecration in 1913

Choirboys wearing surpluses, mid-1930s (left, Rev. Lewarne in a suit, and right, Cecil Prior and Mark Silver; Dennis Harper is the eighth boy from the left)

were two choirmasters, Messrs Martin and Trappitt, and Miss E. Salmon was the organist. Later, Mr Sant of London House Stores was choirmaster.[5]

In 1913, five years after the church was first opened, the parish of Spencers Wood, which embraced parts of the parishes of Shinfield, Grazeley and Swallowfield (all in the Diocese of Oxford), was created, with the church being consecrated by the Bishop on 29 September. Lewarne became the first Vicar and he conducted the first wedding on Easter Monday 1914.[6]

### Through two World Wars

In 1917–19 Lewarne joined the forces for a year as a chaplain and his parish duties were performed by a retired clergyman, Ernest Thoyts (b. 1852 in Sulhamstead), who also gave organ recitals, and according to some notes on the history of the organ, had a beard. 'His Thursday organ recitals were very popular, and always packed the church.' After the return of the Vicar, a Parochial Church Council was set up. Later that year girls were allowed to join the choir, though not to wear cassocks and surpluses, nor to sit in the choir stalls.[7]

The Wedding of Geoff Day and Alice Marcham in 1936/37. On the left is Mr Day (licensee of the Farriers' Arms) and his wife is next but one to him. The groom is Geoff Day (brother of Mr Day) and the bride is Alice Marcham (aunt of Irene Elliott who gave us the photo). The bridesmaid next to the bride is Anita the hairdresser's grandmother. Irene is the little bridesmaid on the left. Irene is fairly sure this was taken about 1936/7 because that was the year her mother died and she thinks her mother was still alive then.

A Social Club was formed in 1921 and 'American teas' (also known as 'Bring and Bite') were held regularly to raise funds. There was a Sunday School and a Girl's Club (between 1925 and 1940), but no club for boys. In 1928 Kenneth James Salmon donated land in Clares Green Road for a Vicarage and as he was an architect he also did the plans for the house. Between 1931 and 1934 there were numerous fundraising events to finance its building. The foundation stone was laid in 1933.[8] Lewarne never married and he had first his sister and later a lady of Russian descent as housekeepers. The picture shows a wedding group outside the church porch, taken around 1936 or '37.

During the 1940s the Sunday School continued in the Village Hall and a Bible Class was also held by the Misses Smith at their own home, Glandfield, opposite the pond. Dorothy Bonney (neé Bennett), who attended the school and then went on to teach, says that there must have been about 100 children. She recalled outings to Burnham Beeches.[9] Gwen Lambourne recalls Sunday School outings to Streatley Hills and Maidenhead Thicket.

Rev. Lewarne in uniform

Interior of the church after electric lighting had been installed: note also the organ, behind the flag on the right-hand side of the chancel

During World War II, soldiers stationed at Stanbury Camp marched to the church for services; after they left for the invasion of Normandy there is no record of the POWs from Stanbury attending church.[10] Rather than black out the church during the war, winter evening services were held during the afternoon. (See Chapter Thirteen for more about the War.)

Electricity had not reached all areas of Spencers Wood by 1939 and further installation was suspended for the duration of the war. During 1946 and '47 the Vicar and the PCC put a lot of effort into raising funds for electric light in the church; this was eventually installed in 1948, after a delay caused by a shortage of labour and materials (compare the picture on page 129 and above, before and after electric lighting had been installed). In this period of austerity, fuel shortages in the winters of 1946–47 and 1947–48 meant that the three-hour Good Friday service had to be cut down to an hour.

Having served as Vicar for 40 years, in March 1953, Lewarne had to retire due to ill health and was presented with £80 and an illuminated scroll. Sadly, he died in July aged 82, and his ashes were buried in the church, a memorial stone marking the spot to the left of the altar. He was evidently a competent and well-liked Vicar who had led his flock through two world wars. 'He was a real village Vicar', according to John Elliott, 'whose presence was keenly felt'.[11]

## Spiritual and evangelical effort

Ross Young Stone succeeded Lewarne as the second Vicar of Spencers Wood. Installed in 1953, he was to stay for nearly 20 years. Stone was an energetic, High-Church clergyman who never ceased to strive for the spiritual improvement of his parish, measured in increases not only of the electoral roll but also of the number of communicants and the number of confirmations. The church building was not neglected, however, and many material improvements and 'beautifications' were made. Indeed, one of the first of these projects was to provide new, iron entrance gates as a memorial to Frederick Lewarne, but this was deferred in 1954 because of the heavy expense of treating woodworm in the organ.

On the spiritual side, early in 1954 Stone announced the first changes: he wanted the bell to be rung for Matins and proposed to celebrate Sung Eucharist at 9.30 each Sunday in Lent. The electoral roll stood at 96, an increase of 34 over the last year of Lewarne's incumbency. The Vicar was pleased with the turnout at festivals and hoped that it would increase on ordinary Sundays.

The following year (1955) a fund was started to buy a processional cross (£27). At the annual parish meeting, the financial position was reported as satisfactory but there were no grounds for complacency as 'the cost of everything is rising'. 'Spiritual life ... had increased, as evinced in the larger number of communions made'. A Young Wives group had been formed, and a new choir under Mr Stephens the organist. A fete was held in and around the Village Hall, for which the grounds had to be cleared: it made £45 9s. 11d., a little more than the previous year. The Vicar and his wife donated a crucifix to hang behind the pulpit. This was the first year of the Michaelmas supper, with community singing among other entertainments. This event seems to have continued to be popular for many years.

## The Sunday School Schism

More controversially, in August 1955 the Vicar announced the reorganisation of the Sunday School: he wanted the older children to meet for a service and instruction in Church, while the younger ones would continue to meet in the Hall. This was to cause a schism: the Sunday School teachers 'would not agree to teach the catechism or to follow any systematic teaching ... they offered to resign'. The Vicar, with the support of all but one of the PCC members, believed that the 'teaching should lead up to preparation for confirmation [and that] the teachers should be communicants'. Miss Dorothy Rogers, one of the teachers, asked for the return of the *Golden Bells* hymn books, which had been bought by them with money raised from carol singing; 'the council ... express disapproval at the way the children have been [literally] led away from the church'. By March 1956, the Vicar had taken over the Sunday School himself, and was teaching about 20 children, who 'are keen and enjoy their lessons'. He regretted that the former helpers 'had not been agreeable to his suggestions and had started up a rival Sunday School'.[12] Miss Rogers joined the Congregational Church, where she played the organ.

### The Free Will Offering Scheme

Fundraising was a perennial issue and, later in 1956, a 'Covenant Scheme' was suggested as a more reliable way of raising funds than the succession of fetes, bazaars, jumble sales and so on. The following year this crystallised into the 'Free Will Offering' scheme, and 400 copies of a letter and 'forms of promise' were delivered to local households. Despite a 'poor response' the first year, this initiative did start to generate income, particularly when it was supplemented by 'income tax rebates' on behalf of donors who fill in a 'covenant'.[13] By 1959 the FWO scheme had 44 subscribers and was described as a 'moderate success'.

### The Jubilee Year

1958 saw the fiftieth anniversary of the dedication of St Michael's. New gates were needed and in July it was hoped that they would be ready in time for Michaelmas (they weren't!) A 'Caledonian Market' and a cricket match were planned to pay for them (although the latter was never held). More excitingly, a goose supper was planned, to which founder members of the parish were to be invited. The Caledonian Market was held on 27 September, with stalls selling produce, books, old clothes, white elephants and refreshments. There was also a children's party with films on 29 September. The goose supper was 'an undoubted success', with 19s. 6d. in hand afterwards (the Michaelmas suppers were not primarily fundraising events). Tickets went for 5s., the four geese were 'dear', having cost £8 from Mrs Clements; the dressing of the geese was done for free and most of the other food was donated. Later that year a line drawing of the church by Mr Walker was used as a Christmas card, which was later reported as 'successful'.[14]

### The 'Mission'

As the 1960s dawned, the Vicar and the PCC were exploring the idea of 'planned giving', with representatives of other parishes coming to speak to them of the successes they'd had with it, both as a method of fundraising without bazaars and so on and as a way of increasing the number of communions and confirmations. St Michael's concluded that it was too soon after the start of FWO and did not meet the aims of 'Christian Stewardship'; instead they set their sights on increasing church attendance by means of a 'Mission'. The PCC brainstormed the problem of attendance: two suggestions were that Morning Prayer instead of the Eucharist should be sung on certain Sundays and that they could hold a 'congregational practice' session to overcome the 'difficulty of unfamiliar hymns'; the 'slowness and difficulty of psalms' was mentioned, as well as the 'possibility of having more ladies in the choir and having them robed'.

Rev. Stone had Sabbatical leave in 1971 and moved in 1973 to be Curate-in-Charge of Aldermaston and Wasing, replaced at Spencers Wood by David Anthony Low. In the dark days of winter 1973, the Boxing Day service was cancelled because of past non-attendance and there were no lights on the trees 'as a gesture towards the national effort on economising on electricity'; attendance at Christmas services was down on previous years. At the annual parish meetings of 1975, however, the Vicar reported 'a year of growth' and again in 1976 another year of growth, with 14 confirmations.[15]

## Too many churches, not enough parishioners

Nevertheless, due to falling attendances, in 1977 evening services were cancelled – 'not a decision made lightly' – and the Vicar of St Michael's also became Vicar of the parish of Beech Hill with Grazeley, helped by an non-stipendiary minister, John Hart. Although this initially caused a further drop in attendances, the 'downward trend ha[d] been convincingly reversed' by the following year. In 1978 the parish ran a 'Stewardship Campaign', the great success of which was due to the chairmanship of Dick Seymour, who was to continue to campaign on behalf of St Michael's for another 30 years. When in 1982 Rev. Low returned to Rochester diocese to be Vicar of St Barnabas Gillingham, he was praised for having revitalised St Michael's, which he attributed to good teamwork. He felt that the 'church was in a strong position to 'take off''. Frederick Simon (b. 1942), was his successor. In May 1985 Rev. Simon moved on and it took nearly a year to find a replacement (the state of the Vicarage being cited as 'having an adverse effect' on prospective incumbents).[16]

Peter Aubry Edwards (b. 1930) was installed in April 1986 and, although his incumbency was to be short, he was very popular. He presided over a period of indifferent finances and attendance numbers. After only five years Edwards retired as a result of ill-health, and services were being taken by a non-stipendiary minister, Karl Wiggins. A draft Parish Profile of 1991 describes the village as having a population of 3500, with 'a preponderance of white, middle class, conservative, agnostics … [the] majority are recent arrivals with the increased technological development in Thames Valley. The average residence time is lower than the national average'. There were 57 on the Electoral Roll – a number that had halved in the past decade – a choir of 'six ladies', a Sunday School attended by 21 children, four teenage helpers and one teacher, Guides and Brownies (Cubs and Scouts were associated with the URC).[17]

The next Vicar (though not an incumbent in the traditional sense), Gerald Oliver Shaw, arrived in February 1992.[18] When he retired in 1997, Shaw reviewed progress since the Parish Profile of 1991 – his words, shown opposite, express, better than an outsider can, the situation he found and the one he left.

A bench was made by Michael Seymour as a memorial to Peter Edwards, and placed in the Garden of Remembrance at the west end of the church in 1993.

### The ecumenical movement

1993 saw the start of an ecumenical movement in the area: interdenominational services – between St Michael's, the United Reformed Church, the Methodists and the Roman Catholic church of Christ the King in Whitley, whenever there was a fifth Sunday in the month – were considered. In September there were discussions between Rev. Shaw and Terry Hinks of the Methodist Church in Three Mile Cross, resulting in a proposal for joint services. This evolved by the end of the year into the 'Local Ecumenical Project', described by Shaw as 'a moving of the spirit, a time for change and a need to work together to be consistent with our mission'. Hinks stated that the 'time had come to be

### The Vicar's view of the 1990s

On arrival in the Parish I found people were tired and suffering from loss and bereavement [Rev. Edwards had recently died] having worked hard and loyally for several years in very difficult circumstances.

This was reflected in the Church Building and grounds. I state this as a fact and by no means as a criticism, in fact it gave a focus for working together and rebuilding on firm foundations laid by my predecessors

Because of the importance and attractiveness of the Gospel and Lord we serve it is important that people approaching the Church see it as a loved and welcoming place.

The grounds and paths were renewed and there has been constant care given to the grass, flower beds and hedging, and a new notice board was installed. People can see that this is a place which is respected and loved.

The Church was physically cold.

> Fortunately the Insurance Company agreed to fund the repair of nearly all of the 70 damaged and missing window panes.

> A new heating system has been installed.

The Church was dark.

> Margaret [Baker] did a marvellous job in making the floor sparkle with new surface preparation.

> A new system of lighting has been installed.

> New Altar Curtains lighten the place.

> New Altar Frontals express the seasons and the joy of worship

> A new Vestment Press has been given for the Vestry

People can 'Hear'

> A new amplification system has been installed

The Church is welcoming

> New carpet has been placed in the rear of the Church in preparation for further development as a 'Social Area'.

The Church is a place for Worship and Joy

> The Choir have introduced new forms and sounds of worship

> Advised on and introduced a new comprehensive Hymn Book

> Assisted in the formation of Family Worship

> The New Common Lectionary will begin on Advent Sunday

The Church is for the Development of Children

> The Sunday School Staff have introduced a new integrated and differentiated scheme of work for Children

The Church is for the Village

> The Grounds are used by the Guides and Brownies, as well the Fete, a 'Village Fireworks' has been established

> More people have chosen to celebrate their baptisms and marriages in the Church – recognising if only potentially but hopefully that God has a place in their lives, because they can see that St. Michael's welcomes and cares.

The Church is a place of Remembrance

> People can now place appropriate memorials to respect the memories of those who have worshipped in this Church

Thank you

It has been a privilege to have been working with people who have given so much of their time, energy and prayers in the service of our Lord.

I have not mentioned particular names or persons because this has been an era of teamwork.

> Gerald O. Shaw, 1997 (Source: BRO, D/P 194/8A/16, Review – progress since the last Parish Profile, St Michael's, Spencers Wood, 6 November 1997).

bold, that we should not be too tentative or too small in vision to capture the imagination. This is not a marriage of convenience but a spirit led action'.[19]

The vision was to build, literally, a 'New Church'[20] and by August 1994 the Declaration of Intent drafted by the Methodists, the United Reformed Church and St Michael's was 'to develop a single joint church centre to be known as [name was never filled in] and to establish a Local Ecumenical Project ['CENTRE' written in above], with the necessary sharing agreement for the building'. It seems that re-purposing St Michael's was considered, requiring:

> [the] reorganisation of sanctuary: a necessary part of the development, to help all feel it is <u>their</u> church and to make the church more suitable for united worship: eg altar/communion table needs to be lower/nearer the people; pews are probably too inflexible; entrance area needs to be developed; aspects of the URC and the Methodist Church need to be incorporated.[21]

It was intended that the Three Mile Cross and United Reformed Church buildings would be sold to fund the development at the larger St Michael's site, the centre opening in 1996.[22] But the Anglican congregation did not have time to decide whether they were in favour of the project before the Methodists declared that they did not wish to proceed: 'there is clear desire among them to retain their own facilities'; and the United Reformed congregation felt that 'it [was] not viable for them without the involvement of the Methodists'.[23]

### Celebration, challenge and unification

Rev. Shaw retired late in 1997 and again it took nearly a year to find a replacement. Joan Hicks arrived in October 1998 as the new Priest-in-Charge. This young, likeable ex-schoolteacher was to forge new links with Ryeish Green School and to start a successful children's choir.[24]

Rev. Hicks was to preside over the celebrations marking both the Millennium and the Queen's Golden Jubilee in 2002. To mark the former, there was a very successful service held in the church on Millennium Eve 1999 and on 7 May 2000 a yew tree propagated from 2000-year old stock was planted. The year 2000 also saw the first mention in the PCC minutes of 'inputting data onto the Web Page for Spencers Wood and Grazeley' and of 'Gift Aid' (a scheme enabling registered charities to reclaim tax on a donation), after the minimum donation limit was removed in the April Budget. The Jubilee was celebrated at the beginning of June 2002 with a Pentecost Picnic at the Vicarage and a special church service.[25]

But being Vicar of Grazeley as well meant that the main Sunday service had to start at 10.30 to allow the Vicar to get from one church to the other:

even so the service often started late; there were complaints about the length of services too. Another challenge of Hicks' period of office was the expense of organ repairs (including the removal of asbestos from the blower box), which ate into reserves.[26]

## Unification with Grazeley

Another undercurrent was the parlous state of both the fabric of St Peter's church at Grazeley and the age and size of its congregation. In 2002 an insurance valuation put the cost of repairs at Grazeley at £100,000 and it was clear that the church would have to close.[27] Complete merger with Spencers Wood parish became the best option and this was to happen before St Peter's was finally closed. This meant that after 13 years of sharing clergy, the PCCs merged into one. The parishes of Spencers Wood and Grazeley with Beech Hill were united on 1 April 2004, with a single PCC elected at the AGM.

## The formation of the United Benefice of Loddon Reach

While this merger was happening, a wider change in the 'Ministry south of the M4' was also being discussed. It was clear that the number of stipendiary clergy in the parishes of Beech Hill, Grazeley, Spencers Wood, Swallowfield, and Shinfield (Reading Deanery) was to be cut from three to two. Several ideas were put forward as to how this could be achieved: the original proposal was that one would be incumbent of the new benefice and the other would have 'a specialist focus on schools work and education'. But a meeting at Shinfield came up with the idea of a team ministry, and this was eventually accepted. By early

The planting of the Millennium Yew: (left, foreground) Tom Bennett, Liz Ratcliffe, Gwen Hayes, Dawn Clarke, Ada Wells (with spade), Rev. Joan Hicks; (right, foreground) Cecil Prior, Rev. Hicks, Tom Bennett, Liz and Ben Ratcliffe, Ross Macmillan (digging), Jackie Blow, Thomas Lloyd (in striped t-shirt), various Rainbows and Brownies. To plant the yew, Tom was chosen as the eldest member of the Church and Ross as a member of the Sunday School.

Rev. Béatrice Pearson (*Loddon Reach*, February 2013)

2004 the name Loddon Reach Benefice had been agreed.[28] The Team Vicar was to live at the Spencers Wood Vicarage and the Team Rector at Shinfield Rectory; Swallowfield Rectory was to be sold.

Joan Hicks moved on from Spencers Wood in January 2005; she was loved by everyone and her ministry had meant a great deal to the local area as a whole. In February 2006 Maurice Stanton-Saringer became Team Rector of the Benefice and, in September the same year, Béatrice Pearson arrived to take up the post of Team Vicar. Both Pearson and Stanton-Saringer retired in 2013. During their time, St Michael's celebrated its Jubilee with a Centenary Flower and Craft Festival and a Centenary Celebration with Confirmation service.[29]

## Changes to the fabric of St Michael's Church

As a modern church, there have not been many major changes to the building itself: from the outside, St Michael's is almost identical to how it was when it was first built; the interior, however, is a different story. Two different requirements drove the changes: the desire for an area for less formal interaction than the original 17 complete rows of pews could offer, and the need for toilets. In 1976 the guiding principles were: 'to bring the congregation closer to each other and to the altar and persons leading our worship' and to provide space for 'formal and informal discussions and small meetings … displays and exhibitions'.

The first principle could not be addressed directly: the problem was that the altar was considered to be too remote from the congregation, way back in the chancel. But they couldn't move the altar nearer the chancel step because the organist and the choir needed to be in sight of each other, and they couldn't move the organ because of its 'condition and the cost that this would entail'. Moving both choir and altar into the

Looking towards the west end of the church: during rewiring in 1981 (*left*) and in 2016 (*opposite*)

nave would have meant losing pews at the front and not being able to create informal space at the back. As a result, four rows of pews were taken out at the back of the church, and half a row at the front, on the right-hand side, to allow the font to be moved from the west end of the church. The west end could then begin to be used for coffee after services, initially a controversial subject. The choir vestry was at this time still in the north-west corner: moving it would have been 'more aesthetically desirable and would have given more space but was not practicable'. However, the removal of pews had the advantage that the congregation had to sit nearer the altar (although not everyone appreciated the benefit of this!) Incidentally, at this time the 'Standing Committee did not see the need for a Car Park as the Village Hall Car Park was convenient and freely available'.[30]

## The building project

In 1991 the lack of toilet facilities were first reported to the PCC as prohibiting a local resident from attending services, but it was not until another ten years had elapsed, that the PCC began to talk about a 'building project'. The proposed building was discussed with the Diocesan Advisory Committee: 'Should we be looking at something slightly bigger, perhaps with kitchen facilities and room for storage? Would secondary access be needed? Should there be a road access and car parking? ... for an extra £5,000 the proposed building could be extended by 1 metre all round'. After a visit to see the new parish room at Sulhamstead, it was clear that the proposed building was far too small to be useful; and would need to be quite tall to balance the architecture of the church, so would perhaps have to be two storeys; the cost would be £100,000 plus £12,000 for car parking facilities. The new building would be very useful for Sunday School, Tiny Tots, PCC meetings, office space and so on, especially in a future with no stipendiary priest and therefore no Vicarage. But this was in a time when the parish was not even paying its way in the diocese: could it raise funds in the wider community?[31]

### A 'room with a loo'?

After two years, applying for planning permission for a parish room was being discussed. It was now referred to as the St Michael's Centenary Project or the 'room with a loo', and £1,200 had been raised. Although the need for a parish room was still felt, in November 2003, the project (now referred to as the 'Church Extension Project') had to be put on hold for six months because of organisational upheaval that was taking place.[32]

In 2005 a £20,000 bequest by a parishioner meant that a scaled-down version of the earlier church room plans could be considered and a planning application for a disabled toilet, kitchen and small meeting room (5m by 4m) at a cost of £40–50,000, was submitted in May. Under Rev. Pearson, this was to evolve into what is now the hugely successful Caf'Active. It was Pearson's idea to get rid of the choir vestry at the back of the church and her determination and single-mindedness about the project that pushed it through. She found a good architect and the parish was lucky to get additional funding from various bodies. The project manager was David Bryson-Richardson.[33]

### The opening of the community café

Caf'Active opened its doors as a community café on 5 May 2010, managed by Debbie Johnson-Wait, and staffed by volunteers. The space above the kitchen and toilet can be used for meetings and storage, and is popular with wedding photographers as it provides a vantage point. The café area itself at the back of the church is also used for meetings and other activities outside opening hours. Let the Vicar's words before the grand opening describe the place of St Michael's in the village today:

> St Michael's is very much a part of the local community, and that's what this café is all about. I meet a lot of people in this job, and young mothers, in particular, were telling me that they wanted somewhere to

Caf'Active,
2016

get together ... it has snowballed from there, gaining a lot of support along the way. I see Caf'Active as an ideal way of nurturing our partnership with the community, and I am looking forward to a future in which we remain at the centre of village life.[34]

### Ryeish Green memorials

In 2012 the Spencers Wood Local History Group was instrumental in making sure that children and teachers who had died during their time at Ryeish Green School would continue to be remembered. While researching the history of the school, we discovered a number of memorial plaques in the grounds of the school – which was to close shortly. With the profits from the sale of books we had them renovated and got agreement to hold a memorial service at St Michael's. The service was held on 15 September 2012: it was conducted by Rev. Pearson and attended by over 50 ex-teachers and former pupils of the school. The memorials are now located against the south wall of the church where the Priors' magnolia tree used to be.

Rev. Paul Willis,
Team Rector
from 2016

### Postscript

Following the retirements of Stanton Saringer and Pearson in 2013, Peter Jarvis was designated Team Rector. Before he took up the post fully he had to stand down, accused of serious offences against young people, offences that were alleged to have taken place before he moved to the parish. Meanwhile, in May 2015, Paul Willis – an ex-RAF trumpet-player who grew up in Sunderland, and moved to Loddon Reach from St Anne's and St Peter's parish in High Wycombe – arrived to take up the post of Team Vicar. In February 2016 Jarvis was convicted, and Rev. Willis became Team Rector. He and his wife Gill live in Shinfield Rectory. Rev. David Little was inducted as Team Vicar in September 2016.[35]

# Notes

1 Geoffrey Tyack, Simon Bradley and Nikolaus Pevsner, *The Buildings of England: Berkshire* (1966, 2010), p. 528; *Berkshire Chronicle*, 3 Oct. 1908; BRO, D/P 194/28/6/1, Appeal leaflet for the proposed church at Spencers Wood, 1907.

2 D/P 194/28/6/4, Form of service for laying of the foundation stone, 1 Jan. 1908; D/P 194/28/6/2, Appeal to complete the nave and chancel arch, 1908; D/P 194/28/6/3 Balance sheet of garden fete and sale of work, 16 July 1908; Tyack, Bradley and Pevsner, *Berkshire*, p. 528; D/P 194/28/6/5 Order of service for consecration of the church, 29 and 30 Sept. 1913.

3 BRO, D/P 194, Spencers Wood Parish Register.

4 D/P 194/28/9, Notes on the history of the organ (n.d.); *Reading Mercury*, 12 Nov. 1910.

5 D/P 194/8/2, Vestry meeting 13 Apr. 1909; memories of Gwen Lambourne.

6 D/P 194/28/6/5, Order of Service for the Consecration of St Michael's, 1913; *London Gazette*, 30 Dec. 1913, p. 9600.

7 D/P 194/28/9, Notes on the history of the organ (n.d. but probably created for an exhibition in 1977, when a photograph showed Thoyts with a beard); *Reading Mercury*, 9 Feb. 1918. D/P 194/8A/1, PCC meeting, 15 Apr. 1920. In the Church of England, in 1921 the PCC replaced the old Vestry committee as the executive committee of the parish. The PCC is responsible for the financial affairs of the church and the care and maintenance of the church fabric and its contents. It also has a voice in the forms of service used by the church. D/P 194/8A/1, PCC meeting, 15 Oct. 1920.

8 Gwen Lambourne. *Reading Mercury*, 27 May 1933.

9 Dorothy Bonney, 'Recollections of Spencers Wood Sunday School, c. 1937–54', in Spencers Wood Local History Group, *Our Village of Spencers Wood* (2001), p. 29.

10 Gwen Lambourne.

11 John Elliott of Three Mile Cross, quoted in Spencers Wood Local History Group, *Our Village of Spencers Wood* (2001), p. 25.

12 D/P 194/8A/2, PCC meeting, 18 Oct. 1955, Annual Parochial meeting, 8 Mar. 1956.

13 D/P 194/8A/2, PCC meetings, 19 Sept. 1957, 6 Dec. 1957.

14 D/P 194/8A/3, PCC meetings, 8 July, 9 Sept., 13 Nov. 1958., 27 Feb. 1959.

15 D/P 194/8A/4, Annual Parochial Church meeting, 10 Mar. 1971, 17 Mar. 1975, 15 Mar. 1976; PCC meetings, 19 Dec. 1973, 20 Feb. 1974.

16 D/P 194/8A/7, PCC meetings, 24 Oct. 1977 and 26 Sept. 1985; Vicar's reports 1978 and 1979. Dick Seymour's association with St Michael's goes back to the 1950s when he audited the annual accounts; he was elected to the PCC in 1960, became its Vice-Chairman in 1962, and Churchwarden in 1963 (D/P 194/8A/2). He was chairman of the Stewardship Campaign until 1986 (D/P 194/8A/7, 16 June 1986). In 2004 he was presented with a Common Worship Lectionary to thank him for his long service on the PCC (D/P 194/8A/17).

17 PCC minutes are missing for the period 1988–90. D/P 194/3/5/3, Parish Profile; D/P 194/3/5/10, Memo from N. D. Sorrill, for the Churchwardens, 1 June 1991.

18 D/P 194/8A/15, PCC meeting, 7 May 1992; a memorial to Peter Edwards is being discussed in the PCC minutes of 25 June, so he must have died around the time Shaw arrived.

19 D/P 194/8A/15, PCC meeting, 29 Apr. 1993, Ecumenical meeting held at the Vicarage, 12 Oct. 1993.

20 D/P 194/8A/15, Ecumenical meeting held at the Vicarage, 25 Nov. 1993.

21 D/P 194/8A/15, Memo from Terry Hinks, Aug. 1994.

22 Ibid.

23 D/P 194/8A/15, PCC Standing Committee, 3 Nov. 1994.

24 D/P 194/8A/16, PCC meetings, 29 Sept. and 18 Nov. 1998; Kate Mitchell, personal communication; D/P 194/8A/17, PCC meetings, 5 Dec. 2001; Lent Group discussion summary 2003.

25 D/P 194/8A/17, PCC meetings, 19 June, 16 Oct. and 7 Dec. 2000, 2 July 2002.

26 D/P 194/8A/16, PCC meetings, 31 Jan. 2000 and 6. Sept. 1999; D/P 194/8A/17, PCC meetings, 5 Dec. 2001 and 11 Feb. 2002.

27 D/P 194/8A/16, PCC meeting, 7 Apr. 1999; D/P 194/8A/17, Extraordinary PCC meeting, 22 July 2002.

28 D/P 194/8A/17, PCC meetings, 30 June 2003 (report on 'Ministry south of the M4'), 4 Sept. 2003 and 19 Feb 2004.

29 Kate Mitchell, personal communication.

30 D/P 194/8A/6, Papers concerning an internal reorganisation of the church building, 1976; D/P 194/8A/4, PCC meeting, 1 Dec. 1976.

31 D/P 194/8A/15, PCC meeting, 21 Oct. 1991; D/P 194/8A/17, PCC meetings, 9 July 2001, 5 Dec 2001 and 11 Feb. 2001.

32 D/P 194/8A/17, Lent Group discussion summary 2003, PCC meeting, 3 Nov. 2003.

33 D/P 194/8A/17, PCC meeting, 17 May 2005; Kate Mitchell, personal communication.

34 *Loddon Reach*, April 2010, p. 27.

35 *Wokingham Paper*, 8 Feb. 2016; *The Register*, 22 May 2015, Loddon Reach Benefice Web site, loddonreach.org.uk/the-team.htm [accessed 5 May 2016]; *Loddon Reach*, Sept. 2016.

## CHAPTER ELEVEN

# The Village Hall

*Margaret Bampton*

Spencers Wood Village Hall, despite its proximity to St Michael's Church, belongs to the residents of Spencers Wood village and has always been run by trustees.[1] Anna Hunter (formerly Anna Carter) had the Hall built in memory of her husband, Henry Lannoy Hunter, who had endowed St Michael's Church in 1908, the year before he died. According to Pevsner, it is 'an unusually handsome village hall of 1911. Arts and Crafts Tudor, with a steep roof, windows with wood mullions under hipped dormers, and tall chimneys'.[2] The architect was Nathan Thomas Salmon (1875–1947), who lived at Eastrop in Spencers Wood and was based in Reading and Wokingham.[3]

Architect's drawing of the Village Hall

The first committee consisted of seven members, who could co-opt others, if they so wished, from the Parish Council. These were the Rev. F. T. Lewarne and S. J. Long who both represented St Michael's Church; M. F. S. Magill and E. G. Mills who were from Spencers Wood Sports and Social Club; E. C. M. Goddard who represented the British Legion in Spencers Wood; A. J. Perce who represented Spencers Wood Congregational Church; and Mrs I. Salmon who represented the Mothers' Union of Spencers Wood.

Anna Hunter died in 1936 and her daughter Mary inherited the Hall. Ownership of the Hall was transferred permanently to the village in 1948, in a conveyance between Mary Hunter and two trustees, namely Maurice Magill and Ernest Mills, of Highlands. At the same time the name officially changed to 'Spencers Wood Village Hall'. Mary Hunter wished it to be used for recreational, educational, social, moral and physical training through the medium of reading and recreation rooms, a library, lectures, and classes and so on.

Tighter rules about charities were brought in 1960 and again in the 1990s, when a new Trust was formed, using the conveyance of 1948 as a basis to allow for 13 members on the committee. There were 11 representative members including two from the civil parish of Shinfield and two from St Michael's Church. The other seven groups represented on the committee were the Monday Club for pensioners, Spencers Wood Badminton club, the Brownies and Guides, the Playgroup, the Toddlers group and the Women's Institute. The committee could co-opt two more members. Rosemary Hollingshead was the person named to convene the first meeting. The Trustees' regulations were and are quite onerous and all the trustees have to know the rules. As usual with

Girl Guides outside the Village Hall, 2007

a committee, there has to be an elected chairman, vice chairman, secretary, and a treasurer. A quorum of one third of members is required for a meeting to continue. No bankrupt can participate and all members have to sign the minutes. All inhabitants of Spencers Wood over the age of 18 can attend the AGM and vote.

The Hall, which holds a public entertainments licence, has always derived its revenue mostly from lettings and also from fundraising. There are restrictions on numbers in connection with its public liability insurance. As well as the groups represented on the committee, over the years other groups have used the Hall for various activities, including aerobics classes, stitching club, multiple sclerosis meetings, a physically and mentally handicapped music group, jumble sales, private parties, discos, fetes, fairs, bingo sessions, dances, sales, village functions and so on.

## *Before the Second World War*

There is little information about the use of the Hall from before the 1940s. Rosemary Holloway can remember receiving a mug for the 1935 Royal Jubilee. The British Legion used to meet there and Rosemary's brother, Alan, was a member. The Legion held a Carnival with a Queen every year and also concert parties. David McMurray's mother appeared in these concerts and they travelled to other venues in Ted Clements' lorry. Reg Norriss can remember going to the dentist there, being marched up the hill from Lambs Lane School in a crocodile for an examination. The dentist used a portable mechanical drill, which was driven by foot as this was before electricity was supplied to the village.

Another memory from this time comes from Marion Pyke, who recalled having ballet lessons from Joan Brooker. Every Christmas, there was a pantomime at the Palace Theatre in Reading and the girls would hope they would be chosen to appear there. Their costumes were made by Mrs Read from Three Mile Cross and Mrs Brooker would choose the girls. Marion has photos of herself holding a tambourine, but when she was about ten, Joan Brooker took her to one side and said that she thought Marion was too heavy to go on her *pointes*. With that, Marion left.

Marion also remembered the Sunday School using the Hall, where they had a party every Christmas. The entertainment was the same each year, with a magic lantern show performed by either Billy or Bobbie's Magic Buttons. They knew exactly what was coming and, once, the lantern (thought to run on gas) blew up and there were flames and much smoke. Earlier than this, Cecil Prior remembered belonging to a Drama Club called 'Our Village' and Mrs Ethel Lowe remembered performing in the Hall with her daughter, Olive. Sometimes the performance was at the Village Hall and at other times at the Institute, behind the Congregational Church. The Sunday School would also have concerts in the Hall.

### The Second World War and after

During the War, the Hall played many roles, providing entertainments for the troops from Stanbury, as well as housing an ARP (Air Raid Precautions) post and providing a base for the Home Guard. According to Cecil Prior the ARP post in the Hall was manned day and night throughout the War. Ruth Drinkwater said that her eldest brother served in the Home Guard as his poor eyesight meant that he was not allowed to join the regular army. John Winder was also in the Home Guard during the war and remembered that they would march from the Village Hall, in uniforms and carrying rifles, to Highlands where, at the Lodge (opposite the end of Hyde End Road, now demolished), there was a camp with camouflage. Mr Silver who lived there would tie firecrackers onto the end of a rifle and pulled a string to set the crackers off because they had no bullets. The camouflage caught alight once and caused havoc. John Elliott received £5 from the villagers' War Gratitude Fund and started a youth club with part of it.

Other activities were whist drives, concerts and dances. Dotti Johnson and her sister Patricia, can remember film shows powered by generators as there was no electricity until after the Second World War. Soon after the First World War, a Women's Social Club had been started, running every Thursday from 7 to 10 p.m. The ladies would have a whist drive first, followed by a dance, in which they danced old-fashioned ballroom dances, the music being provided by a pianist. Other groups, such as the Nursing Association or the Conservatives, would have whist drives followed by dances and they would first play 24 rounds of whist, which lasted until 10 p.m. The young people would arrive at the Hall around 9.30 p.m. for the dancing, which went on until one in the morning.

At the far end of the Hall, where the stage is today, the men had a billiard table, usually partitioned off. When there was a concert, the stage had to be erected over the table and taken down again afterwards. The billiards club declined and eventually the table was removed and a permanent stage erected in its place. When the Village Hall committee required some cash to install a telephone in the Hall, Cecil Prior very generously gave them a cheque for £75 for its installation. In the 1960s, the drama group from St Michael's requested that the stage scenery be kept under the stage rather than stored on top. The group originally used to store it elsewhere, which must have been awkward. To light the exits at performances, the group would use bicycle lamps.

The Clinic in the Village Hall: its opening by Mary Hunter and other pictures

During the 1960s, the Baby Clinic transferred here from the Library building (see Chapter Nine). Dorothy Cripps has provided several photographs, showing the opening of the clinic, the new clinic store opened by Mary Hunter in the shed at the back of the Hall, children enjoying a party and a group of people outside the Hall.

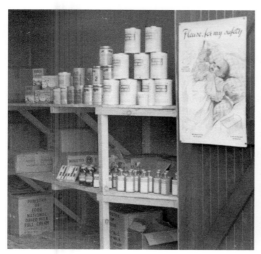

For most of the 1960s, the committee was concerned about the draughtiness of the Hall. Early on, one member said that now they had new electric heaters there could be more dances as the excuse of draughts had been eliminated. But the heaters were put on a meter, which discouraged their use. The concerts put on by the OAPs had shown that the lighting was defective and the committee needed to contact the Ministry of Social Services to add another electrical installation. Social Services were required for the regulation and maintenance of the Hall. Two more heaters were installed four years later. There was a draught at the back door and a curtain was made using the leftovers from the stage curtain material. In 1967, the windows at the back of the stage were boarded up and double-glazing and weather-stripping were discussed and then installed. But the heating problem continued and the committee decided to have oil-fired heating installed at a cost of £147, by Messrs B. C. Tucker (Heating) Ltd; the oil cost at the time was 1s. 6.2d. per gallon. After this there is no further record of draughts in the minutes, although to this day people still complain about how draughty the Hall is.

There were many repairs and maintenance works during the 1960s, including worm treatment and repairs to the porch, at a cost of £79, which was a lot of money then. The roof required mending and the roof on the shed at the back needed re-covering in corrugated iron, for which the Congregational Church paid. The outsides of the Hall were painted, the kitchen modernised, and the toilets renovated. The decoration was spruced up, fire extinguishers were purchased, new hogging was put on the car park, new flooring was purchased, a connection was made to the main drainage in 1964, redundant gas pipes were removed, and the hedge and lawn were cut by the Play Group organisers. In 1970, there was a distribution of leaflets to the villagers explaining that the Hall was self-supporting and asking for donations towards the cost of extending it. Four contractors supplied estimates ranging from £2,500 to £3,700, and the lowest, from Mulhern and Son, was accepted. A grant was received from the Department of Education of £1,228 and the rest of the money was raised by increased lettings, and various events during 1972, including a play, an arts and hobbies exhibition, a jumble sale, a square dance, a fashion show, a lecture on the Far East, with slides, a Reading Phoenix Choir concert, another fashion show, a barbecue, a bazaar, and a fancy dress dance. The dances often exceeded £100 profit, dancing to bands such as Len Parr at 13 guineas (£13 13s.) per event, J. Read and his band, at 22 guineas (£23 2s.) per event, and Mr Brooks' band at 15 guineas (£15 15s.). Henry Jelliman played at the Village Hall with his skiffle group called the Green Lights. Dorothy Edwards used to run a fete on the 'Rec' (recreation ground) every year, and held dances with a brass band in the Hall for the benefit of people suffering from muscular dystrophy.

Winter
Wonderland

When the new stage was erected in 1961, the performers produced *A Winter Wonderland* with a party for the children from Lambs Lane School. Performances before this had been staged on rickety tables stored along the sides of the hall. There were two performances of *Snow White* with different leading ladies. Many children appeared in these productions and some names are David, Christine and Isabel Winter; Jill Winder; Fay Parsons; Joanna and Felicity Morrison; Jane and Derek Evans; Daphne Seymour; Margaret Biggar; Carole Astle; Audrey and Elaine Taylor; Jane and Alex Seago; Claire Beatty; Ronnie Clark; Cherry, Thomas, Robert and Andrew Kempton; David Fontaine; and Margaret Sheerman.

The play, in January 1972, was called *Boeing-Boeing* and was produced by the St Michael's Players. The cast consisted of Caroline Angus, Philip Seymour, Helen Angus, Anthony Druce, Alison Grainger and Judith Colledge. Behind the scenes were Colin Clipstone, Tim Walford, Janet Walford, Peter Knapp, Dor Evans, Philip Seymour and Richard Stone. Philip Seymour directed a play about Mrs Beeton. He also wrote and directed plays and entered the competition for One Act Plays in the Shinfield Festival. One was *Ring Around the Moon*, another, *The Happiest Days of our Lives*, and a third, *A Resounding Virtue*. His last play, *Thomas*, about Thomas à Becket, had three performances in St Michael's Church. Audrey Sizer was the pianist for the performances.

In 1971, Miss Hunter, the Hall's benefactor, died and flowers were sent to her funeral. During the previous decade, the following people had provided

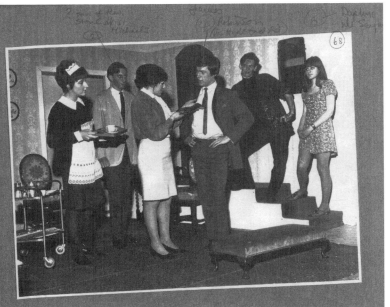

Play scene, late 1960s/early 1970s. Second from left, Richard Stone; third from right, James Robinson of Hyde End Road; right, Daphne Seymour

Programme for *Thomas*, 1970s (*right*)

## THOMAS

(The Life of Thomas Becket of Canterbury)

by PHILIP SEYMOUR

### CAST

| | |
|---|---|
| THOMAS BECKET | BRIAN HODGKISS |
| HENRY II of ENGLAND | ROGER ING |
| FITZURSE | GORDON TAMS |
| DE TRACI | PETER WALMSLEY |
| DE MOREVILLE  Barons | JOHNNY FERRAND |
| BRITI | STEVE COOK |
| FOLIOT, Bishop of London | GRAHAM HUBBARD |
| ROGER, Archbishop of York | PHILIP MORGAN |
| HENRY, Bishop of Winchester | RICHARD STONE |
| HILARY, Bishop of Chichester | JOHN HODGE |
| HERBERT of BOSHAM  from Becket's | ANTONY DRUCE |
| A SERVANT  court | RICHARD JENKINS |
| JOHN of SALISBURY | MARTIN BARNSDALE |
| GRATIAN, envoy from the Pope's court | DAVID ORMEROD |
| STANDARD BEARER to the King | JEREMY COLLIS |

| NOBLE LORDS and MONKS | IAN YOCKNEY | RICHARD PARKES |
|---|---|---|
| | ROBERT HARRISON | JOE GIBBS |
| | PETER HUTT | GERALD BURGESS |
| | JOHN FORD | MICHAEL DANIELS |
| | JOHN LAYTON | ERIC OSBORN |
| | DAMION KNOWLES | IAN ARCHIBALD |

The Play produced by PHILIP SEYMOUR

### PRODUCTION STAFF

| | |
|---|---|
| Stage Director | Colin Clipstone |
| Wardrobe | Ali Grainger |
| Lighting | Paul Drayton |
| Sound Effects | Nick Blandy |
| Continuity | Dee Grainger |
| Make – up | Lesley Holdsworth |
| Properties | Daphne Seymour |
| | Antony Druce |

### ACKNOWLEDGMENT

The Players wish to express t appreciation to the Rev. R.Y.S for his help and advice to Moffatt and the Willink Co Secondary School for their with costumes. Pierre Edmunds

assistance to the Hall: Mr Michael Barber, Mr Jones, Mrs Morrison, Mrs Blackwell (salaried caretaker and cleaner), Mrs Parkes, Mrs Gelston, Miss Clements, Mr Curling, Squadron Leader Gibbs, Mrs Anders, Mr Jarvis, Mrs Dor Evans, Rev. Stone from St Michael's, Miss Ethel Bullingham (the booking clerk), Mr John Salmon, Mrs Magill, Mrs Askew (who had been an actress at one point), Rev. Griffiths, from the United Reformed Church, Mrs Green, Mrs Prankard (the butcher's wife), Mrs Taylor, the wife of the Headmaster at Lambs Lane School, Mr Histead, Mrs Janet Rickson, Mr Dyer, Mr Linfoot, Mr Richards, Mrs Rollason, Mrs Frona Hyde, Mrs Lorna Merry, Miss Betty Robertson, June Jenkins, Mrs Biggar, Mr and Mrs Bob Winter, Mr Philip Seymour, Mrs Joan Clipstone, Mrs Wilson (a silver birch was planted in her memory), and Mr Walford.

One fundraising event was the ever-popular Easter Parade for children, which was started by Jackie Blow and Penny Paylor in the early 1990s. It was initially held on the recreation ground and they had a cowpat draw. Squares were drawn on the field and a pantomime cow dropped a pat into one of them. In other years the Spring Fair has taken its place and recently it has seen a Zumba class demonstration. Other children's events were discos in

May and at Halloween, as well as pyjama parties. A time capsule was buried by Lambs Lane School at the Hall to commemorate the Millennium. Sadly the Hall suffered from a lack of volunteers during this period and required rescuing from oblivion. Jackie Blow, who is an energetic charity fundraiser, has raised funds for the Hall in many ways, by holding fairs, barbecues, skittles, table-top and jumble sales, film shows, bingo, baby clothes markets, and dances. In return Jackie has been able to use the Hall free-of-charge for raising funds for the 2000 Mozambique floods, the Thames Valley Air Ambulance, and the 2004 Tsunami appeal which raised £1,745: a remarkable achievement.

Time capsule buried by Lambs Lane School at the Village Hall at the Millennium

Spencers Wood Local History Group Open Day, 2005

In 2012, there was great excitement when a travelling company from the Watermill Theatre and Oxford Playhouse, put on *Some Like it Hotter*, a spoof on the 1950s film, *Some Like it Hot*. A drama group has put on enjoyable productions. The Hall has been used for furniture and carpet sales, a war games group, band practices, birthdays and other anniversaries. Spencers Wood Local History Group held many exhibitions and film shows here to fund our first book.

There are few days when Spencers Wood Village Hall is unused; it is a valuable resource to the community, but it still needs volunteers and local support. Long may it thrive.

## Notes

[1] This chapter is based on the following sources: Spencers Wood Village Hall Minutes, 1961–1971; Village Hall Extension Appeal, 1971; Conveyance, 1948; Information Pack for Spencers Wood Village Hall Management Committee members; Charity Registration, 1991 (all in the possession of the Village Hall Trustees); *Loddon Reach*; *Junction 11*; and the memories of Jackie Blow, Ruth Drinkwater, John Elliott, Dor Evans, Rosemary Holloway, Dotti Johnson, David McMurray, Reg Norriss, Cecil Prior, Marion Pyke, and John Winder.

[2] G. Tyack, S. Bradley and N. Pevsner, *Berkshire* (The Buildings of England, 1966, 2nd edn. 2010), p. 528.

[3] A. Brodie *et al.*, *Directory of British architects, 1834–1914* (2 vols, updated and expanded edn, 2001), II, p. 528.

# CHAPTER TWELVE

# Lambs Lane and Ryeish Green Schools

*Update by Mary Wheway*

## Lambs Lane School

Berkshire County Council established Lambs Lane School following the 1902 Education Act and it was opened in 1908 as an all-age school that could take 234 pupils. It was positioned at the northern end of Swallowfield Parish so that it could accommodate pupils from Spencers Wood and Swallowfield. The school in Swallowfield closed at this time and its pupils were transferred to Lambs Lane.

The first Headmaster of the new school was Mr John Russell, who had previously been Headmaster of the school at Swallowfield. He remained at Lambs Lane until 1925 when Mr Arthur David took up the reins. Conditions in a rural school like Lambs Lane were sometimes difficult: the school was heated by an inadequate boiler and pupils often complained of feeling cold. Gas lamps supplied lighting, because mains electricity did not arrive until after the Second World War.

During the Second World War the school took in evacuees, some of whose memories can be found in Chapter Thirteen.

Great changes took place after the 1944 Education Act: Lambs Lane became a primary school and the older pupils from all the local schools went to a newly opened secondary school in Ryeish Green, which had previously been an all-age school as well.

Mr David retired in 1948 and Mr Reginald Taylor was appointed Headmaster, but facilities were still not very good at the school. There was no main drainage for the toilets and the washbasins were troughs with a supply of cold water only. The juniors had one long trough for washing and the infants had a smaller trough. The boiler frequently broke down and would provide little or no heating or hot water. The kitchen was far too small to cope with the extra numbers staying for school dinner, and the playgrounds, which had been resurfaced before the war, had not been done well and were beginning to crack and break up. The school had no connection with a telephone system.[1]

There were many improvements in the 1960s: main drainage, hot water, new toilet blocks, a new hall and kitchen, a telephone connection and, in 1966, the school field on the opposite side of the road was purchased.

On Mr Taylor's retirement, Mr Ivan Webster took over but he only stayed for three years. Mrs Marion Evans became Headmistress in 1969 and introduced team teaching into the school. When she retired in 1985, Mrs Margaret Stevenson became Headmistress, a popular appointment as she had previously taught at the school. She oversaw the introduction of the National Curriculum. After Mrs Stevenson retired, Mrs Sharon Finn became Headmistress and she is still in post, taking the school into the twenty-first century.

## The School at Ryeish Green

When the school first opened in 1910, it was known as Shinfield Three Mile Cross Council School and it catered for children from five years to school leaving age. There were 81 pupils registered at the school in April 1910.

Mr Reely was Headmaster of the school for 27 years until he died in office, when his Deputy, Miss Lambourn, became Headmistress. At the same time the county decreed that the school should just teach children aged five to eleven years. The older children went to the senior departments that remained at Shinfield, Lambs Lane and Grazeley. Two years later, the school began to receive evacuees and the upheaval was too much for Miss Lambourn, who resigned with ill health.

It took two years for the education authority to find a new Head, but Miss Beck was eventually appointed in 1943. The school went through a difficult period under her leadership and numbers fell. After the 1944 Education Act, the county decided to make this school Ryeish Green Secondary Modern School, with some improvements to the building, and appointed Mr Nation, previously the Headmaster of Farley Hill School. He was a much-loved Headmaster, who died in 1963. Mr Gillard succeeded him, taking the school through to 1971 when he retired.

It was at this time that another big educational innovation took place, the introduction of comprehensive schools. Mr

Further details of the history of the school and many pictures and memories of former pupils and staff can be found in our publication, *The History of Lambs Lane School.*

Veale, the new Headmaster, and his staff worked very hard to bring the school up to standard and, although they were at first denied a sixth form, they immediately set up an unofficial one. The school expanded and eventually funding for a sixth form was provided by the local authority.

Ian Marshall took over the leadership of the school in 1992, followed by Mrs Jenny Garner in 2001, but from 2006 Mrs Garner was faced with the difficult task of overseeing the closure of the school: Wokingham Borough had decreed that Ryeish Green School should close and that local children should be bussed to other schools in the borough. The school was run down gradually until it closed in its centenary year, 2010. Local parents were incensed by this decision and a small group tried in vain to save the school. Then central government started a new policy of providing direct funding for 'free schools', thus by-passing local education authorities. A committee was formed to set up a free school here at Ryeish Green: this opened in 2012 as Oakbank School, using the buildings first opened in 1910.

More details of the history of Ryeish Green School, together with pictures and memories of former pupils and staff are to be found in our publication, *Celebrating the Centenary of Ryeish Green School.* And the story continues in Chapter Fourteen, 'Oakbank School'.

### Note

[1] BRO SCH/19/8, School Log Book.

# CHAPTER THIRTEEN

# Our Village in the Second World War

*Margaret Bampton*

From 1936 Hitler was seen to be taking steps to retrieve those lands that Germany had lost after World War I, so the British government started doing what it could to protect the country in case of another war. Air Raid Precautions (ARP) were put into operation as early as March 1938 when the Home Secretary asked for volunteers. By September 1938, more than 1.5 million volunteers had begun to prepare for war by carrying gas masks and identity cards. ARP wardens could be identified by their blue tin hats with a white W on them.

Throughout 1938 the subject of Air Raid Precautions keeps coming up in the minutes of Shinfield Parish Council: they want to know what methods are to be adopted. In 1939–40, the Council recorded that the Air Ministry had closed a footpath leading to RAF Shinfield Park, and later another footpath was diverted by the National Institute for Research in Dairying (NIRD) in Shinfield. In February 1940 the minutes record that Mr Clements had offered a store at Clares Green as a mortuary for civilian deaths and the building that now houses the Spencer Wood Library was designated as an emergency centre. It was around this time that Cottage Hospitals were set up for local emergencies. A siren was erected in the centre of the village opposite where Waring's bakery is today. A request for sandbags was referred to Wokingham Council, as was a stirrup pump for the Parish Clerk for emergencies and wool to knit 'comforts', such as gloves and balaclavas, for the troops. The County Comforts Committee was very soon abandoned, although no reason was given.[1]

The Home Guard was set up in 1940 as another part of the civil defence and continued until 1957, when it was disbanded. Pillboxes, which were concrete gun emplacements in a hexagonal shape (resembling the boxes medical pills came in, hence the name), were built on a defensive line, the 'General Headquarters Line' or 'GHQ Line', which started from London following the River Thames. This line was the second most important (after the coastal defences) of over 50 such lines in Britain, and it was designed to protect London and the industrial Midlands; it curved towards this area from where the River Loddon joined the Thames at Charvil near Twyford, skirted Swallowfield, and continued round to the point where the Loddon reached the Kennet and Avon Canal at Burghfield. Along this line, to strengthen the defence, were tank traps, one of which was at the Foudry Brook, Grazeley, behind Stanbury. After heavy rainfall the local children would swim in these tank traps but they wouldn't tell their parents. There were also pillboxes at Foudry Brook, Benham Drive and Loddon Court Farm and they can still be seen today.[2]

Pillbox at Benham Drive

Meat, dairy products, eggs, sugar, and so on were rationed, and nearly everyone grew vegetables to supplement their diet. Many people kept chickens and their surplus eggs were collected to send to the troops. Mrs Magill at Highlands was the County Co-ordinator for the collection of eggs. Excess fruits were bottled or made into jam for use during the winter. Sometimes they were sent to the Co-operative Jam Factory in Berkeley Avenue, Reading, for general use. Children would also collect rose hips for syrup and acorns to feed all the extra pigs that were kept.

Clothing was also rationed and clothes had to be purchased using coupons because of the short supply of materials: it was a case of 'make do and mend'. Stockings were made of rayon or lisle which was not very elegant, but nylon was relatively new, and scarce because of the war, and only the lucky few could get hold of fashionable nylon stockings. Some women went bare-legged, colouring their legs with watered-down gravy powder with a drawn pencil line up the back of their legs, to simulate nylons with their back seams! Beryl Odell recalled having renovation lessons at Spencers Wood Library (the local emergency centre), where they were taught how to turn worn-out sheets sides-to-middle and how to patch them, to make them last longer, and how to make pillowcases from the good parts of worn sheets. Socks were darned and shirt collars were taken off, turned over and sewn back to make them last longer. Elbows on jackets were patched.

Railings and other scrap metal were collected to be turned into ammunition and equipment and two scrap metal dumps were established – one at Grazeley Road, Three Mile Cross, and one at Shinfield Green. The following year, in 1941, two stewards were needed to take care of the dumps because the metal was being

164 RAILWAY OPE[R]

Sept

The 164 Railway Operating Co. RE at Stanbury

stolen. The school at Lambs Lane collected for the Spitfire fund and Vic Earley recalls that a mile of pennies was laid from the Post Office in Spencers Wood to the one in Three Mile Cross. Adults sat on chairs set evenly apart, keeping their eyes on the pennies then collecting them up when the task was finished. The value collected was £220 and contained 52,800 coins. Other projects were undertaken to help with the war effort, such as the 'Dig for Victory' campaign, where every available space was dug up for vegetables and so on. The formation of a 'Pig Club' was discussed by the Parish Council in 1940.[3]

Military vehicles on their way to Aldershot would pass through the village almost daily, preceded by a dispatch rider, and according to Rosemary Holloway, the soldiers would always wave to the children. Sadly, when the survivors of Dunkirk passed through they were all too exhausted and weary to wave. Pat Hollinshead, an evacuee, on her way back to Lambs Lane School from lunch at the Library, had her first sight of black American soldiers. This must have been after America had been brought into the war when the Japanese bombed Pearl Harbour in late 1941. Pat said that they were absolutely charming and were as delighted as the children were to stop and chat. 'Christmas came early' that year when they gave the children 'candies' and chewing gum. Pat's family lived in Riseley in a bungalow that had a corrugated roof, four rooms, an outside privy complete with bucket, a black-leaded stove for cooking and heating and a cold water tap. When Pat's father eventually joined them, because he was in the Fire Service he would stay overnight in the Brigade's HQ in Highlands farmyard. Although he was 42, he was called up and sent to Australia.

In 1942, Spencers Wood Common and all the way down to Swallowfield was full of Canadian Troops prior to the raid on Dieppe. Peter Bennett, another

young evacuee, was out collecting conkers, when he fell out of a tree and broke his arm. He was taken to Battle Hospital in Reading, which was full of wounded Canadians after the unsuccessful raid. Several local women married Canadians, including Iris Waldron, who lived in The Square. Iris was unable to travel to Canada after the war to join her husband because of illness. She – and her father – died a few years later from tuberculosis (TB). The Royal Engineers (REs), 164 Railway Operating Company (shown in the photo above), were also at Stanbury, as were the Pioneer Corps who guarded the Prisoners of War (POWs). The 164 Company is difficult to trace. It may have been a Canadian or British Company as both countries had REs. Reg Norriss said that the REs would sometimes attend church parade at St Michael's. On hearing a thud, the soldiers once told Reg Norriss that a parachutist had landed nearby on his way to Burghfield Royal Ordnance Factory (ROF), where Mrs Norriss, Reg's mother, worked. Maybe this was the German airman that Enid Fisher's father, the village policeman, captured in the woods. A child was asked about local airfields by two adults who were probably looking for Woodley aerodrome.

Many local people were in 'reserved occupations', which meant that they were not called up for the armed forces because they were more valuable at home, providing essential services to keep the country running. Marion Pyke's father, Carol Hyde was a car mechanic, which was a reserved occupation, and he was detailed sometimes to go to France to mend the army lorries and tanks that had broken down. Her grandfather was in the Home Guard. Marion said that Swallowfield Park sheltered some of London's Museum and Guild Hall treasures for safety, even though the house was greatly neglected. Reg Norriss, who lived in the North Lodge of Stanbury, became an apprentice at Vickers

Armstrong in Reading after he left Lambs Lane School. They made fuselages in Station Road, wings in Vastern Road, tail planes in Caversham Road and in Thatcham they made fuselages and wings. All these pieces were taken to an airfield to be assembled. William Baggs worked for Mr Grover, a local builder, during the Second World War, fitting gun emplacements at Slough, and only coming home at weekends.

The photo below shows a tree felled by the crew of Judd's Sawmills. Someone has carved a large V sign on it, followed by the Morse code for V. We can date this picture to after June 1941, when the opening notes of the movement known as 'Fate Knocking at the door' of Beethoven's Fifth Symphony – which

'A moment in time during the War': the crew of Judd's Sawmills, Spencers Wood. This photo was donated by Andy Skipp, grandson of Harold Howells, the man on the left with his arms folded. Note the 'V', the Morse code, and the words 'Hitler's Coffin'.

just happens to sound like the Morse code for V – were first introduced on the radio as an aural version of V for Victory. Below the owner's initials (HWG), someone has carved the words 'Hitler's Coffin'.[4]

David McMurray's father, James, was in the REs at Stanbury and David's great uncle lived in Weathercock Cottages on the estate. Another great uncle, Ted Staniford, lived in the South Lodge and worked on the estate. David's mother got exemption from the Land Army because she had lost her mother and had to look after her father and brothers. Even so, she worked at Burberry's in Reading making greatcoats for officers and was there when Reading was bombed: the factory girls dived under the tables. Reg Norriss witnessed the bombing from the top of Spencers Wood Hill. The aircraft that bombed the People's Pantry, a restaurant in Reading, apparently used the A33 as a guide to get there; it was shot down by anti-aircraft fire the same day, crashing at Saltdean, near Brighton.

Women worked hard in factories, shipyards, engineering, hospitals, and on the land, wherever they were needed to replace the men who had gone to war, but they were exempted if they had large families, were pregnant or had children under 14. Women without children could be conscripted for the National Services. By 1943, 90 per cent of single women and 80 per cent of married women with children over 14 worked. After the war, the women, particularly the married ones, lost their jobs, so that the men had work to come home to. Many, however, did not return to agriculture and this created a shortage of land workers.

The Miles Aircraft factory was in Basingstoke Road, Reading, near the Gillette factory and in 1943, Brian Kite worked there after he left school. Local people were used to seeing unusual planes, such as a 'Flying Pig' or a 'Canard', flying from Woodley airport, and they were mostly Miles Magisters or Masters painted bright yellow to show they were training aircraft. Whilst fire watching on the Miles factory roof, Brian once saw a flying bomb fall and explode on a farm in Earley. Where Junction 11 is now, Brian can remember an anti-aircraft rocket device manned by the Home Guard, which was, however, never fired in anger. Brian's family were evacuees: as a child he would often cycle out to Swallowfield and in later life, after he had served his time in the RAF, he came to install an amplifier at Motor Trade Machinists, which was opposite Spencers Wood Post Office. To his surprise he was reunited with many who had worked at Miles.

Many local people enlisted and Peter Middleton was in the Parachute Regiment sent to Palestine. He ended up in hospital in Egypt. He was one of only two British men in the ward. He recalled a German POW there who had a brother at Stanbury POW Camp. When Peter came home he asked the Camp Commander if the POW could visit him and he was allowed to. In 2002, Peter was still in touch with one of these two German brothers.

Colin Hearn's father worked at Ford Bros in Shinfield before joining the Royal Army Service Corps (RASC) for the duration of the war. He rejoined Ford's afterwards, before taking on the garage in Three Mile Cross.

John Elliott's family certainly contributed to the War. His eldest brother, who was with the Marines, was unfortunately killed; another brother was at Dunkirk and a third was taken prisoner in Italy. One of John's jobs after demobilisation from the Navy in India, was to convert the huts at Stanbury into living accommodation for the homeless and those on council house waiting lists.

### *More Memories from Evacuees*

The Women's Voluntary Services (WVS) – founded by Lady Reading in 1938 – organised the evacuation of children from the cities to rural areas, to keep them safe from the bombing. The members of the WVS wore a green uniform and they ran nurseries, rescue centres and canteens, helping homeless people with shelter, food and water. Some went abroad in 1943, initially to Algeria and Italy and then to every combat zone in the war. Some 240 women were killed and a Roll of Honour exists in Westminster Abbey. More information about evacuees can be found in our Centenary histories of Lambs Lane and Ryeish Green Schools.

Most homes had to receive evacuees unless they paid a fine. Nancy Hutchinson was away in Devon when war broke out and on returning home found two evacuees under ten living there. Mary Parish said that there were two at her grandparents' home in the village and her aunt ran an infants' school during the war called Little Sunbeams School, which was overcrowded with children. The family of Ron Holyday (who was not born until after the war) came to Spencers Wood as evacuees to escape the Blitz: they stayed with Ron's grandfather who was a baker at Philpott's (now Waring's Bakery) and already had one evacuee. Ron's mother worked for Woolworth's in Reading and would cycle there from Spencers Wood every day. She would leave her bike at Watt's Cycle shop for 1s. per day. Everyone kept chickens and some kept pigs. There were pigs on the allotments (where Diana Close now is) in Beech Hill Road. An aunt of Ron's would visit Spencers Wood and play the piano at the Red Lion.

One of the three evacuees that stayed with Barbara Baker's family in Riseley returned to London because she was homesick and was then killed in the blitz whilst at the cinema.

Another evacuee who went to Riseley School was Rita Clarke, whose father worked at Woodley aerodrome. They first moved to the Five Bells public house in Riseley; then they lived with Mr and Mrs Smith in a thatched cottage; and finally moved to Wyvols Court, on the road to Basingstoke, where they lived in the stableman's quarters at the rear. It didn't have a toilet and Rita slept on a camp bed in the one bedroom, which the whole family of four shared. The water came from a well and because they didn't have any electricity, they used oil lamps for lighting. Her mother found that wearing her gas mask was useful whilst peeling onions! Rita's father was in the Fire Service which met in the pub but didn't have a fire engine. A Mr Oliver ran the estate at Wyvols with Beryl, the Land Girl, a member of the Women's Land Army, which was formed in 1939. The Land Girls helped farmers turn over an extra six million acres to agriculture, but they had a rough life, hedging, ditching, laying land drains, muck-spreading and so on, and although they were seen as doing a grand job, as women they were paid much less than men.

Brian Terry, who was evacuated to Highlands for most of the war, tells two stories, about the Auxiliary Fire Service (AFS) and the Home Guard.[5] Both of these organisations were run from Highlands because it was the only large house that hadn't been taken over by the army. The AFS possessed an ancient Dennis fire engine with solid tyres and an escape ladder. It was red with lovingly polished brass fittings, but it was to be painted a battleship grey. Then the old engine had to go, to be replaced by a Coventry Climax trailer pump towed behind a suitable vehicle. The Area Officer, a professional fireman, would arrive in his Rolls Royce to drill the volunteers. One day he arrived in his car, now painted the same grey colour, and announced that the Rolls was to be their new Auxiliary Towing Vehicle, or ATV for short, until another ATV could be found. Spencers Wood had the only fire brigade that attended fires in a Rolls Royce! Eventually the real ATV arrived and was used to attend fires in Southampton docks but, later, London fire fighters arrived in Spencers Wood and took the place of the locals. The Londoners lived in a hut in the farmyard of Highlands and made it their home-from-home. One night during 1941, German bombers were heard and the

Fire Brigade stationed at Highlands during the Second World War. The fire engines are visible behind them. Left to right, back row: – Steer (lived in Grazeley), Gilbert White, Harold Waite, Percy White, –, –, –, Geoff Day, Bill Clements, Vernon Burchell, Les Seymour; Front row: –, Bill Appleton, Mrs Mills, John Mills, Harold Booth, Charlie Turner, Horace Bacon

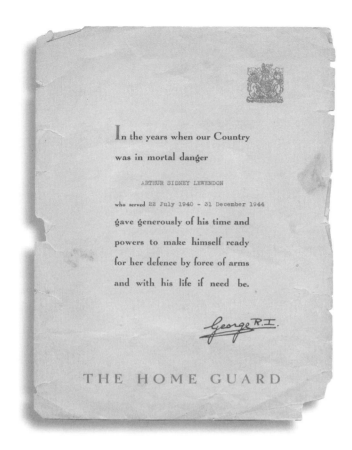

In the years when our Country
was in mortal danger

ARTHUR SIDNEY LEWENDON

who served 22 July 1940 - 31 December 1944

gave generously of his time and
powers to make himself ready
for her defence by force of arms
and with his life if need be.

George R.I.

THE HOME GUARD

Home Guard
Certificate for
Arthur Stanley
Lewendon

siren sounded. The next day the lawns surrounding Highlands was covered in white patches, where incendiary bombs like those in the London blitz had fallen. They could have caused much damage, as they did to many cities and ports, but because the AFS was at Highlands they were dealt with quickly. The bomber had dropped what was called a 'Molotov Breadbasket', which consisted of a large, cylindrical case filled with the incendiary bombs. These devices were dropped by parachute which, when opened, dropped all the little bombs over quite a large area. The casing and parachute from the device were put on show in St Michael's Hall, as it was then known, with other items of interest. A small charge was made to see them, which went to the Spitfire Fund. Ruth Drinkwater's mother obtained some of the parachute silk to make clothes.

There was a WAFS for women and another organisation called the Supplementary Fire Party of Firewatchers who aimed to put out fires caused by bombs before the blazes grew too big. The AFS was superseded in 1941 by the National Fire Service, which continues today.

The Home Guard, also run by Mr Magill of Highlands, asked Brian Terry's mother for her old pram, which she'd used for her youngest son, Mick. The local blacksmith (possibly Mr Double) fashioned a deck on the springs with suitable brackets to hold the pride of the unit, a First World War Lewis gun. The men paraded with a great deal of swank with the youngest member, Hines' butcher's boy, aged 16, pulling the gun.[6]

### Prisoners of War (POWs)

Enzo Andreini, an Italian POW, worked at Highlands from 1942, probably stationed at Mortimer Camp, which was at Little Park Farm on Beech Hill Road, but after Mussolini's surrender in 1943 Italians were no longer prisoners of war and he went home. Brian Terry became very fond of Enzo, who taught him the rudiments of Italian; they formed a strange alliance. According to Brian, the POWs also carved figures, mostly religious ones, from wood found during their hedging operations and from soap. The prisoners made monkeys on sticks and baskets that were sold to the villagers of Riseley.[7] Barbara Baker said that they would pass the POWs digging a trench in the lane when she was going to Riseley School and was frightened of them initially but as she got to know them she became less so. They were always singing and one song she recalled was 'Lily Marlene'. Other prisoners worked at the sawmill run by Judd and on Body's Farm (then known as Spencers Wood Farm) in the Basingstoke Road. An Italian POW, called Peter, made slippers from twine he picked up on Dawn Clarke's father's farm in Ryeish Green. Suttons Seeds in Reading, took on POWs, both Italian and German, and were pleased with their work, but a shortage of bag-tying string and cord was discovered and the missing supplies were traced back to the camp, where it was being used to make men and women's slippers. It was one way that the prisoners could earn a few pence, as they received very little, and the money was used to buy warm clothing such as gloves. Occasionally, the guards of the Pioneer Corps from Stanbury would raid the huts and confiscate the baskets or other goods that they found. In 2014, Spencers Wood Local History Group learned from Javier Marambo that his grandfather Domenico Marambo had been a prisoner at Stanbury during the war, but unfortunately we could learn no more about him.

The Stanbury Camp was not set up until 1944/45 and one German POW from there, called Walter Drexel, worked in the garden of Ann Carter's aunt who lived in Windsor. He was bussed there by Smith's Coaches of Reading. Ann lived in London during the war and because she collected stamps, Walter gave Ann's aunt two envelopes dated 1947, with German stamps on them for Ann's collection. These were addressed to Walter at Stanbury and came from the Russian sector of Germany. When Ann (coincidentally) moved to Spencers Wood the envelopes came home.

Two envelopes posted to Stanbury house for Walter Drexel

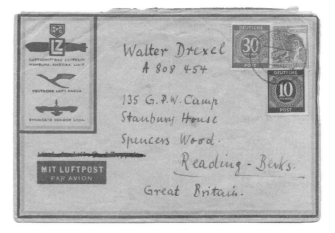

Hans Fischer

Another POW who had a story to tell was Hans Fischer. Aged 19 in 1945, he was captured in the Ruhr by British and Canadian troops. After some hard days without food and water he was taken first to Ostend and then to Tilbury. Hans' first impression of Britain was not very good, but a train ride to Kempton Park changed his mind as the train had upholstered seats: he had been travelling in goods wagons before this. He was interrogated about being a Nazi but he was too young to really understand. From Kempton he went to Oxford where he was given porridge and raisins to eat, which he thought was heaven. There he joined a theatre group and put on a show for the British soldiers. After a year, he was sent to Mortimer tented camp where he worked for the Thames Conservancy and was sent out in a boat to cut down some trees. The POWs lingered at their enjoyable task and helped the lock keepers. After another year at Mortimer, Hans was sent to Spencers Wood where, because he could speak English, he was given the job of waiter in the Officers' Mess at Stanbury. The kitchens were at the back of the house where two cooks and two waiters looked after the Officers' Mess and the Sergeants' Mess; the dining room overlooked a view of Grazeley. Hans had to wear a uniform of a grey army jacket with a coloured circle and diamond in blue or yellow sewn on the back and on the lower part of the trouser leg. The Italian prisoners wore a brown uniform with the same badges. There were about 400 prisoners in this camp and they were housed in the Nissen huts at the side of the house and down the drive towards the Basingstoke Road. They had porridge for breakfast; bread, cheese and black tea for lunch; and whatever was available during wartime rationing for dinner. They were able to have a piece of slab cake once a week, which they looked forward to immensely.

It wasn't until 1948 that the Germans were allowed to go home and it took another year for them to save up enough money to do so. Hans worked for six months to save up, buy some clothes and return to Germany. He originally came from Hanover but because it was so badly damaged, his mother had been evacuated to Turingen in East Germany (note that the envelopes pictured belonging to Walter Drexel, came from Turingen). Hans managed to smuggle himself into the Russian Sector to see his mother but the conditions were so bad he smuggled himself out again. He decided to return to England and for a while stayed at Wistaria Cottage in Three Mile Cross. From here he worked first at Burghfield Road – at a tomato nursery near the old Co-op in Southcote – and later in a Biro factory in Woodley. Despite the years of war, Hans said that he found that the ordinary English people always wanted to help him and were friendly. He married and spent many years living in Caversham.

Another POW at Stanbury, Herbert Heinemann, has written a book about his life as a prisoner but he doesn't say much about Stanbury except that he enjoyed 'listening to the radio broadcasting "Music while you work" every morning with predominant lovely evergreens I was fond of'. He was there in 1948 from January to May on his way home. His main experiences were in Yorkshire and he too was very much taken with the English people. Heinemann's article includes the picture below taken in 1964, of the Stanbury House Camp huts.[8]

POW section photo of Herbert Heinemann War-time Nissen huts in 1964 (Photo taken by Herbert Heinemann)

The POWs were allowed to come and go as they pleased, according to John Winder, and the locals often played table tennis with them. We know that they formed a band that performed at the Village Hall and they also used to attend church and chapel: many villagers remember, with nostalgia, their beautiful rendition of 'Holy Night, Silent Night'. The German prisoners were kept here until 1949 so that they could be debriefed before returning home as many were believed to be Nazis. Some married local women, including Joan Gilman, Gwen Miles and Vera Hatton.

## After the War

As the war progressed and the Allies regained North Africa and then Italy and Sicily, the troops advanced across Europe gaining a victory there in 1945, in May. Peace came to Britain and the mopping up began. Brian Terry had left school before the end of the war, and returned to London to work. With the peace in 1945, he was given two weeks' holiday and he came back to Reading, to stay with those he had known whilst in Spencers Wood. Brian can remember celebrating the end of the war in Europe dancing around the band stand in Forbury Gardens with what he thought was the entire population of Reading.[9] It was at this time that the Americans dropped bombs on Hiroshima and Nagasaki, and the war was finally over. In 1950, Shinfield Parish Council wanted to show the parishioners of Shinfield, Grazeley and Spencers Wood a film about the atomic bomb. Whether they did or not, we don't know.

Mine blocks were removed at Hartley Court Bridge later in the war. In 1944, the Parish Council needed to write to the Officer-in-Charge at Stanbury House as he had 'borrowed' a small lawn mower and tennis court marker from the groundsman at the Recreation Ground.

There was a Home Guard Camp at Bridge Farm in Arborfield Road, near to the Magpie and Parrot public house and, in June 1945, the contents were sold. These consisted of 8 timber galvanised huts, a marquee, 12 bell tents, electric light plant, 40 palliasses, corrugated iron, garage doors, bins, pale fencing, coppers, cutlery, wireless sets and a 'terraplane' motor car. By this date there was obviously no further need for this camp.

Many evacuees, POWs and soldiers have stayed in or returned to the area. The centenary celebrations of both Lambs Lane School and Ryeish Green School were attended by many evacuees, who had provided their memories for our two books, as they have for this book.

## Notes

[1] BRO, CPC 110/1/5, Shinfield Parish Council Minutes, 1937–1951, 17 Mar. 1938, 28 July 1938, 27 Oct 1938, 31 Aug. 1939, 28 Sept. 1939, 28 Mar. 1940; 9 Sept. 1943; 29 Feb. 1940, 29 May 1941 ('the Woodwork centre … now being used as a Communal Feeding Centre'), 30 Jan. 1941; 27 Feb. 1941.

[2] Berkshire County Council, *Bastions of Berkshire: Pillboxes of World War II* (Babtie Public Services Division, n.d.).

[3] CPC 110/1/5, 27 June 1940.

[4] Diane DeBlois and Robert Dalton Harris, 'Morse Code V for Victory: Morale through the Mail in WWII' (paper given at Smithsonian National Postal Museum, 2008), http://postalmuseum.si.edu/symposium2008/DeBlois-Harris-V_for_Victory-paper.pdf.

[5] Brian Terry, *The Days Were Always Sunny* (unpublished, copy in possession of SWLHG).

[6] Ibid.

[7] Ibid.

[8] Hullwebs History of Hull, www.hullwebs.co.uk/content/l-20c/conflict/ww2/memoirs/herbert/herbert-01.htm

[9] Terry, *Days Were Always Sunny*.

## CHAPTER FOURTEEN

# Oakbank School

*by Sarah Codling*

Afer the closure of Ryeish Green Secondary School in July 2010, families in the villages to the west of Wokingham experienced issues with secondary education provision: difficulties gaining places at the school of their choice, long travel times to schools out of the area and no continuation of friendships formed at primary school as local children were dispersed across the borough to a number of different secondary schools. Local residents felt at a disadvantage when trying to gain places at local authority schools due to the oversubscription criteria of distance. In 2010, Wokingham Borough Council held a public consultation to address the issue of secondary school catchment areas across the borough.

Conscious of the issues they faced, a group of parents arranged to meet at a local pub one evening. Many of them had never met each other before but each shared a common concern about the lack of provision in the area and wanted to discuss how best to communicate the local feeling at the consultation. They decided to organise a campaign to raise awareness of the consultation and urge local parents to lobby Wokingham Borough Council and communicate their dissatisfaction with the catchment areas. Unfortunately in spite of their efforts, when the findings of the consultation were published in 2011, it became apparent that the need for secondary school provision would not be addressed by the local authority.

By this time, the parent group had dwindled to a handful of people. They felt that the only alternative was to consider something more drastic and considerably more time-consuming. They were aware of the government's new Free School initiative which made it easier for charities, educational groups, teachers and parents to get involved and start new schools. The new schools would have the same legal requirements as academies, provide genuine parental choice and drive up standards in education.

The group began learning the processes to ascertain whether they could fulfil the local need for secondary education themselves. They named themselves the West of Wokingham Parent Group (WoWPG) and set about speaking to the

Oakbank School

local community to establish whether they would support a campaign to open a school and if so, the type of school they would like.

So began many months of standing at school gates, at local fetes, at any community event, with clipboard in hand, speaking to local residents about the aim of the campaign and asking for support. It was vital to obtain the backing of local parents but also of the wider community in which any prospective school would be situated. In many ways, what the group were trying to achieve was new to the English education system but their vision for the school itself was actually very traditional: a small community school with a strong pastoral ethos and high academic ambitions for every student. With these elements in mind, the group created their vision for the school:

> Oakbank – an outstanding and happy school where all students are empowered, through knowledge and self-confidence, to take responsibility for themselves and their community.

During this time, the parent group partnered with CfBT Education Trust, a not-for-profit organisation specialising in education. The trust would provide the educational knowledge and expertise required to deliver the school. The group was also fortunate to have established links with members of Shinfield Parish Council. The council were very supportive of the campaign itself as they recognised the benefits that a secondary school in the area would offer. From the very beginning Jacqui Barnes and Angela King in the SPC office were personally very helpful, offering information, local knowledge and advice to the group on a wide range of issues.

Over the months, the proposal was written, outlining every detail of the future school including the curriculum, the staffing requirements and the proposed site. After researching the local area, it became apparent that the most logical site would be the disused campus of the old Ryeish Green School. Although in need of refurbishment, the site offered a significantly more cost-effective and environmentally friendly solution than building a new campus from scratch.

The name 'Oakbank' was found when studying some old maps of the area. The school site itself sat on land previously known as Oakbank Farm, which was named after the bank of oaks situated along the perimeter of the land, originally planted during the 1800s when oak was still needed for shipbuilding. The group felt that 'Oakbank Secondary Free School' would be an apt name, in recognition of the history of the grounds in which the proposed school would be situated. Subsequently, the names of the school buildings across the campus were similarly named after other local farms in the area: Hopkiln, Searle, Smallmead, Parrot, Crocker and Floyer.

Community spirit was strong as the group received offers of help and support. Local parent and graphic designer Barney Firth of Cream Design offered professional assistance *gratis* and worked with them to create the overall branding of the school as well as designing the oak leaf logo. He also helped to design marketing and school literature including the first prospectus. Other community members delivered leaflets through letterboxes, members of Shinfield Community Volunteers served refreshments at the campaign public meetings and there was spiritual support from the congregation of Shinfield Baptist Church.

Community involvement was always at the heart of the creation and long-term aspirations of the school. The traditional African proverb, 'It Takes a Village to Raise a Child', struck a chord and was adopted as a slogan for the school. The basic meaning that a child's upbringing is a communal effort seemed appropriate for what local residents were trying to achieve for the children of their community. Another phrase frequently used was 'Of the community, by the community, for the community' to foster a genuine feeling of ownership for local families.

In May 2011, the 200-page proposal was submitted to the Department for Education, accompanied by a petition signed by more than one thousand local residents and letters of support from local stakeholders. The high level of support received from the community was overwhelming and provoked comment by the DoE officials at the time.

It was a long wait for the wheels of bureaucracy to turn but, finally, on the 10 October 2011, it was announced that the West of Wokingham school proposal had been approved by Secretary of State for Education, Lord John Hill. The school would open in September 2012.

Over the following months, work continued in earnest to set up the school for the subsequent academic year. A recruitment process saw the appointment of Mr Nick Dorey as Principal, as well as all the Heads of Department and other teaching and support staff.

There were some issues in securing the Ryeish Green site but after many months of negotiation with Wokingham Borough Council, the site was finally signed over just six weeks before the school was due to open. During the additional months of standing empty, the buildings had been dreadfully vandalised, with every window smashed, internal walls destroyed and central heating pipes pulled from the ceilings. The project to make the buildings fit for purpose was enormous but there was no alternative but to forge ahead. Building contractors Willmott Dixon, who were assigned to the project, worked around the clock, with shifts through the night to complete the campus in time for September.

The House System was to play a major part in the pastoral ethos of the school. There were many thoughts about who each house should be named after: prominent local historical figures, contemporary icons, British pioneers. In the end, Mr Dorey put forward four names that he felt appropriate to head the houses. They were Marie Curie, Edmund Hillary, Helen Keller and Nelson Mandela. Each had come from rather unexceptional beginnings and could have been described as relatively ordinary at eleven-years-old. However, all four had gone on to overcome enormous adversities and accomplish extraordinary achievements. It was agreed that these four figures could be truly inspirational to the eleven-year-old students embarking on their education at Oakbank. To mark which house a student belonged to, they would wear a school tie with a stripe of their respective house colour: yellow for Curie, blue for Hillary, green for Keller and red for Mandela.

It was a proud day for the founders, staff, students and community as Oakbank opened the doors to its first cohort of students on 5 September 2012. The school would receive its first intake of Year 7s and build up with four forms of entry year on year until at full capacity, at around 560 students. This would be considerably smaller than other secondary schools in the area but the figure was based on addressing the local need for secondary education together with delivering the strong pastoral ethos of a small community school.

The school motto was chosen by Mr Dorey as 'Challenge, Commitment, Community'. Students were encouraged to challenge themselves in order to get the most from their education, to show 100% commitment to all aspects of their school life and to enrich the community by using their talents and by caring for and supporting others.

On 10 October 2012, the school held a Founders' Day to mark the first anniversary of the day approval had been granted. It was a day of shared

The Founders of Oakbank, from left to right: David de la Rivière, Shannon Nolte, Sarah Codling, Louise de la Rivière, Jayne Soanes (CfBT Education Trust), Madeleine Young, Yvonne Maxwell-Billing, Sarah Beardmore

celebration as many of the people who had provided help and support throughout the project were there. Representatives from the Department of Education and The Right Honourable John Redwood MP were also present. An assembly was held with performances by each class. Each founder was presented with a folder containing messages from the students:

> Thank you very much for all your hard work. I don't know what school I would have gone to if it wasn't for Oakbank. I really like this school.

> Thank you for all your hard work to make this school happen. It's a real success. Thank you for turning this vandalised building into a masterpiece!

> I would like to say a huge thank you to the Founders of Oakbank for working long and hard to get this school opened and to give the children of Spencers Wood an amazing new school.

> Thank you for founding a great school. It's really good and I like the teachers, the chairs and tables and all of the facilities.

> I am having a great time at school. I have learnt lots. I like the lessons. I also like the uniform. It was nice to come here with some of my friends. Oakbank is the best!

The local press and media took an interest over the course of the campaign. There were regular articles printed in local papers such as the *Wokingham Times* and the *Reading Chronicle*. In addition, there were reports on local news programmes, the BBC's *South Today* and ITV's *Meridian News*. In addition, some members of the parent group were interviewed on the national magazine programme, *The Politics Show*.

In December 2012, journalist John Harris visited Oakbank to research an article that questioned the Free School initiative in general, as well as those compelled to use it, but he admitted that Oakbank had changed some of his preconceptions. He went on to publish two articles for *The Guardian*[1] and for *Shifting Grounds*, in which he wrote:

> Towards the end of last year, I visited four Free Schools... But the most interesting school I saw was also the least remarkable: a new secondary in the Berkshire village of Ryeish Green, near Wokingham, established thanks to a campaign by the West of Wokingham Parent Group, and run by the CfBT Educational Trust. I met two of the parents involved, Sarah Codling and Louise de la Rivière, who were not the pushy, pro-Tory caricatures of lefty demonology, but two women whose demands for a new local school had seemed pretty much unanswerable, and whose central involvement – along with other local parents – in what was now happening said something very powerful. Put simply, if anyone is co-producing a public service, they are. ... When I visited, it was only a couple of months old, but its sense of community and pastoral care was obvious.

The school was becoming well established and had received its second cohort of students in September 2013. Unfortunately, in November Mr Dorey became unwell and after some time and careful consideration, he made the decision to resign as Principal. For a short period, the school was led by CfBT Trust Governor Alex Biddle and then from January 2014, by Interim Principal Andy Kilpatrick OBE. Although Mr Kilpatrick was running Oakbank very effectively, this was a difficult time for a school still in its infancy so it was essential that a permanent Principal be appointed as soon as possible. Over the course of the following term, the vacancy was advertised and the school received many very impressive applications for the post. After shortlisting, a rigorous two-day interviewing process took place. Candidates were interviewed by panels of founders, governors, staff and students. By the end, the decision was unanimous across the panels and Mrs Maggie Segrove was appointed as new Principal of Oakbank.

In March 2013, it was announced that Oakbank would be oversubscribed for September 2014, only its third year in operation. This was the clearest justification yet for the school's creation and testament to the local community who had backed it.

In September 2014, Mrs Segrove took up her post as Principal with a full complement of Year 7 students, writing:

'A small school with big ambitions' was the phrase in the advert for the role of Principal at Oakbank that swung it for me. Once I had read those words, I was hooked. I loved Oakbank from the minute I read about it; being appointed Principal of this community school is the highlight of my career to date.

The staff and students of our school are incredible. I have been overwhelmed by the positivity, community spirit and passion they all have for the success of our school. The vision I have is the same as that of the Founders – a community school which has high aspirations for its students. Oakbank provides quality first teaching which inspires a thirst for learning. We create an environment where learning is not just about what happens in the classroom but about the lifelong memories that the journey through school will create. We want to work with the whole community to grow and develop the global citizens of the future.

It's a real privilege to be sharing Oakbank's amazing journey with our students, our staff, our parents and our community.

Mrs Maggie Segrove BA (Hons) PGCE

Mrs Segrove, Principal of Oakbank

As each year passes, the school will continue to grow in terms of students and the teaching and support staff to sustain it. The creation of Oakbank has been an incredible journey: frustrating, heart-warming, exhausting and rewarding in equal measure! There is a board in the school with a photo of the founders and a brief history of how the school was created. The final wording sums up their story:

Oakbank would not exist today without the overwhelming support and enthusiasm of the whole community; not least the parents who put their faith in the school by enrolling their children as students.

This is what happens when a community pulls together.

## Note

1 *The Guardian*, 4 Jan. 2013 (www.theguardian.com/education/2013/jan/04/free-schools)

# Oakbank School: *Postscript 2016*

Under the very capable leadership of Mrs Segrove and her team, Oakbank continued to thrive. In June 2016, the school received a visit from HMI Ofsted and were delighted to receive the resulting judgement that it is a Good school. The inspectors praised good practice across the board with effective leadership, the quality of teaching, learning and assessment, outcomes for pupils, and personal development, behaviour and welfare.

A few excerpts from the report include:

*The school is a tight community. Relationships between leaders, staff and pupils are very positive and there is a warmth and generosity of spirit which shines through.*

*Parents are very positive about the school and recognise and appreciate the improvements made. In particular, they value the leadership of the principal and the supportive, caring learning environment. One parent said: 'My daughter is incredibly happy at the school. She is thriving socially and academically and has a very positive attitude to learning.'*

*Pupils are encouraged to think for themselves through skilful questioning and they set to work quickly and eagerly. They are given demanding work to do and they rise to the challenge. They enjoy working together and the strong relationships between peers and between teachers and pupils result in faster progress.*

*The compulsory 'Widening Horizons' programme for all pupils at the end of the school day is a key feature. The skills and understanding that pupils gain from these experiences prepare them well for life in modern Britain.*

*Pupils' social, moral, spiritual and cultural development (SMSC) is at the heart of Oakbank's philosophy. The school has a strong moral purpose and pupils are expected to give back to their community.*

*Pupils told inspectors they were glad they chose to come to Oakbank. They like the small size and the community feel. One pupil said: 'We're all so close, like a family.'*

**Ofsted June 2016**

The report demonstrated that the founding vision and principles of the WoW Parent Group – for a school with the community at its heart, providing a rigorous academic curriculum and a strong pastoral ethos to every student – were indeed a reality.

*Sarah Codling*

# Spencers Wood Local History Group

## Margaret Bampton

I have always been an avid reader and collector of books, particularly those about the history of Reading and Berkshire as I was born and bred there. We moved to Spencers Wood in 1982, and I joined the Group when Jeremy Saunders set it up in the 1990s because I wanted to learn more about the area that Mary Russell Mitford wrote about. I learned about Mary whilst at Kendrick School. Miss 'Ghastly' (to differentiate her from 'Juicy') Jones would be amazed at my interest in history, which was nil then, and that Mary made such an impression. Obviously something went in. During the 1990s Kendrick celebrated their 120th anniversary and I suggested that the school should produce an anniversary booklet comprising two sections of 60 years each. The first part would be a reproduction of the first 60 years and the second a compilation of pupil's memories echoing the first part. The task was assigned to me as I had suggested it. This then led to the production of our first village book using memories, so that many people are involved. I hope you all enjoy our second village book as much I have in being involved with it.

## Jackie Blow

I have been living in Spencers Wood since 1986, always knowing that my paternal Grandmother lived here as a child. So when the opportunity came to be part of a local history group it seemed an ideal way to find out about the village and more about her time here. I have been researching my family history for many years and on forming the group, Margaret Bampton and I found we

were distantly related. Then more recently while researching with Jeannie Brice for Chapter Eight, I found a family connection with the Wheeler family, the local builders who developed much of The Square. I have enjoyed interviewing residents for their memories and taking photographs before more changes happen.

## Barry Boulton

I was born in Shinfield nearly 70 years ago and raised by my maternal grandparents whose ancestors had lived and worked in the village from the early 1700s. Although moving to Whitley Wood Road when I was aged four years, I still maintained links to the village through Cubs and Scouts where I became a Queen Scout in 1961 and helped run the Youth Club. The lanes of Shinfield, Spencers Wood, Ryeish Green and Three Mile Cross were my playground.

Twenty years ago, I started researching my own family history and this has led to an interest in local and social history. As my family had lived in the village for so many years, I have found that many of my related families had lived in Shinfield for more than 400 years. My six times great-grandfather made shoes for the charity school. I found this out when transcribing the charity school's Trustees' Accounts that cover the period 1706–1838. I researched, wrote, designed and published *A Walk around our Village* with the Shinfield Local History Society. I love old documents and have helped transcribe Parish Registers and Poor Law Records for the Berkshire Family History Society as well as recording Monumental Inscriptions. At present I am researching trades, occupations and businesses in the area and have gathered material on the servicemen of Shinfield and information on the farms of Shinfield, Grazeley, Three Mile Cross and Spencers Wood.

### Jeannie Brice

Moving into the area and seeing a display at the Carnival, I joined when the group were editing the *History of Lambs Lane School*. On the strength of that book we were invited to write the history of Ryeish Green School to celebrate its centenary. Unfortunately this coincided with the closure of the school, and we were able to advise them about depositing their archives at the Berkshire Record Office. Moving the memorials of the children who had died whilst attending the school, to St Michael and All Angels, was particularly rewarding. Working for a technology company I was keen to help to set up a Web site, to spread the word to people who had moved away, and in 2010 www.swlhg.co.uk was born! The people and stories you hear are incredible! The one that will stay with me forever is a private invitation from Marion Pyke, born and educated locally, taking a ceremony in the chapel of Edward the Confessor at Westminister Abbey. You can hear from Marion on our Web site.

### Sarah Codling

I am one of the founders of Oakbank. I live in Shinfield and have two children – my daughter started at Oakbank in 2013 and my son will join in 2017. Together with two of my fellow founders, I continue to be involved with the school and am immensely proud of its place in the community.

### Catherine Glover

I moved to Spencers Wood in 2012, having previously lived just outside the New Forest. At the time, I was still writing my dissertation for the MA in Regional and Local History at the University of Winchester, but joined SWLHG as soon as I'd finished it. I'm still involved in researching the history of the New Forest, and am also a free-lance copy-editor and Web designer. My enjoyment of living in Spencers Wood has been greatly enhanced by researching its history.

### Patricia Green

After I moved to Spencers Wood in 1972 I noticed how the pace of new building increased, while the village managed to retain its countryside setting. This prompted me to join the Local History Society and become involved with our research and publications. Meanwhile I followed the progress of the many (often major) planning applications, and worked on *A Vision for Our Villages Character Statement*, which was published in 2008, and subsequently contributed to the *Shinfield Parish Community Plan*. Now I am involved with the *Shinfield Neighbourhood Plan*, which will become a statutory part of background planning considerations for new future development. It will be interesting to continue researching and recording the history of the village while watching it change with new housing and its infrastructure.

### Richard Hoyle

I came to Reading in 2000 to take up a post as Professor of Rural History at the University of Reading, but found my way to Spencers Wood only in 2012. More recently I have been Professor of Local and Regional History in the University of London. As a teacher and researcher in local history, I find writing about the places in which I live irresistible.

### Lesley Rolph

I have lived in Spencers Wood since 1989 in an Edwardian house close to Lambs Lane Primary School. My first contact with Spencers Wood Local History Group was around 2006, when I mentioned to them about the poor condition of the school's bell tower. Jackie Blow from the group suggested that perhaps Shinfield and Swallowfield Parish Councils might be able to offer some form of funding to help with its restoration. Their contribution helped start the school's restoration project for the bell tower, which was successfully completed in time for the school's centenary celebrations in April 2008. (For further information about the history of the school, please refer to our book, *The History of Lambs Lane School, 1908–2008*.) More recently I have become interested in encouraging younger people to learn about local history and have created a Junior Historians' Box, which has proved to be a popular addition to our stand at local events.

## Mary Wheway

My interest in history and latterly with local history grew with age. When I retired I wrote down my memories of my Primary School, then I wrote a booklet about a fire at my Grammar School in the Midlands. This caused a lot of interest and led to several reunions. With the 'bit' between my teeth, I tackled the history of Beech Hill Baptist Chapel and also Ridgeway Primary School, Reading where I had taught for 30 years. I joined the SWLHG in 2004 and have been active in the production of three books for the group, helping with the research and writing and also setting them up for publication.

Left to right: Barry Boulton, Lesley Rolph, Jackie Blow, Catherine Glover, Mary Wheway, Margaret Bampton, Jeannie Brice and Patricia Green (photo: Simon Kemp).

# Acknowledgements

Spencers Wood Local History Group would like to thank the many residents, past and present, who have helped so willingly, through interviews, discussions and written memoirs, to provide an insight into life in Spencers Wood in years gone by. We are also grateful to the helpful and patient staff at the Reading Local Studies Library, the Berkshire Records Office and the Museum of English Rural Life. We acknowledge the kind permission given to reproduce images, as follows:

pp. 5, 6, 22, 41 (centre), 76 (top) and 79 (top), Reading Central Library.

pp. 7, 9, 48, 49, 51, 53, 112, and 128, the County Archivist, Berkshire Record Office.

pp. 28 (top), 29 (top), 63 (bottom), 89 (bottom), 101 (centre) and 129, the Museum of English Rural Life, University of Reading.

p. 56, Margaret Baker.

pp. 58, 60 (right), 62 and 67, Rosemary Holloway.

pp. 72 and 83, © Historic England, reproduced under licence.

pp. 74 (bottom), 131 (bottom), 132, 158 and 163 are from the collection of Barbara Debney and we reproduce them by kind permission of her family.

p. 76 (bottom), Gordon Young.

pp. 84, 88 (top), 92, 102 (bottom) and 131 (top), John and Irene Elliott.

p. 97, Anne Wigmore.

p. 98 (top, left and right), Roger Colebrooke.

p. 99 (centre), Beryl Ballauff.

p. 108 (centre), Peter Roberts.

p. 111, Mr Salmon of Spencers Wood.

p. 113 (top), Betty Salmon.

p. 130 (top), Vic Earley.

p. 130 (bottom), Dennis Harper.

pp. 140 (top) and 143 (bottom), *Loddon Reach*.

pp. 145, 149, 164, Dorothy Cripps.

pp. 151, 152, Dor Evans.

p. 160, Andy Skipp.

p. 165, Ann Carter.

p. 167, *WW2 People's War*, which is an online archive of wartime memories contributed by members of the public and gathered by the BBC. The archive can be found on the Web at bbc.co.uk/ww2peopleswar.

Catherine Glover drew the maps and map overlays on pp. vi, 6, 7, 8, 81 and 82.

All other images reproduced in this book are either original photographs taken by members of SWLHG, or images with no copyright owner. Every attempt has been made to discover copyright owners. We give our apologies to any who have been missed and undertake to make amends in any subsequent edition of this book.

# Index